Searching for Islamic Ethical Agency in Post-Apartheid Cape Town: An Anthology

Published by AFRICAN SUN MeDIA under the SUN MeDIA imprint

First edition 2019

ISBN 978-1-928314-61-5
ISBN 978-1-928314-62-2 (e-book)
https://doi.org/10.18820/9781928314622

Set in Palatino Linotype 10/12
Cover design, typesetting and production by AFRICAN SUN MeDIA

SUN MeDIA is a licensed imprint of AFRICAN SUN MeDIA. Academic and prescribed works are published under this imprint in print and electronic format.

This publication can be ordered directly from:
africansunmedia.store.it.si/za/home (e-books)
www.africansunmedia.co.za

Volume XIII in the Beyers Naudé Centre Series on Public Theology

SEARCHING FOR ISLAMIC ETHICAL AGENCY IN POST-APARTHEID CAPE TOWN

AN ANTHOLOGY

Aslam Fataar

SUN MeDIA

Dedicated to the memory of al-Shahīd Imam Abdullah Haron

on the 50th commemoration of his martyrdom

I wish to thank the Beyers Naude Centre at Stellenbosch University's Faculty of Theology, especially Professors Len Hansen and Dion Forster; and Prof. Nico Koopman, Vice-Rector – Social Impact, Transformation and Personnel, for their support with the publication of this book.

The Arabic transliteration was done by Mawlānā Mthokozisi Ebrahim Maseko with the support of the National Research Foundation of South Africa (grant reference number (UID) 85397) through Prof. Abdulkader Tayob from the University of Cape Town. I thank them for their support.

I acknowledge and thank all my friends, teachers, colleagues, and students for their encouragement and intellectual support during many years of friendship, activism and conversation.

I dedicate this book to my wife, Najwa, who lived through every moment of its gestation and writing, and my children, 'Imādah and Sa'eed, whose post-apartheid childhoods provided the provocations for the thoughts expressed herein. Thank you for your love and support.

1. CONTENTS

2. FOREWORD

I am delighted to write this Foreword to an excellent collection of *khuṭab* (sermons, sing. *khuṭbah*) and published articles crafted by Prof. Aslam Fataar, whom I have known for most of my adult life.

The compositions brought together in this book began a quarter of a century ago in 1994, with the onset of South Africa's non-racial democracy, and in one way it may be viewed as the critical observations of an 'organic intellectual' engaging the exigencies of life during the first 25 years of South Africa's democracy.

The book's compositions are presented in chronological order, so the reader is able to follow the ebb and flow of life in post-apartheid South Africa. It is also fitting that the book commences with an excellent sermon about the Reconstruction and Development Programme (RDP) that was delivered at the Claremont Main Road Masjid (CMRM) in 1994, since the core of the compositions are sermons which were delivered here. These were all outstanding sermons, as those who witnessed their public performance can attest to. Their inclusion in this book thus provides a wonderful opportunity for a wider audience to benefit from Prof. Fataar's profound insights.

Prof. Fataar, through his own personal journey and commitment to justice, has developed the unique ability to consistently and courageously convey the call 'to speak truth in clear terms to power'. This is one of the central messages that runs throughout this rich selection of essays and is best illustrated in his CMRM sermon commemorating the 20th annual celebration of Human Rights Day delivered on 21 March 2014. In this sermon he lauds the wisdom and uncompromising witness for justice by Advocate Thuli Madonsela, who at that time was serving as South Africa's Public Protector. He calls on all South Africans to embrace "the wisdom" of Thuli Madonsela and recommit themselves to a politics of engaged democratic citizenship in the service of social justice.

It is thus fortuitous that, after completing her term of office in 2016, she subsequently joined the Faculty at the University of Stellenbosch, where Prof. Fataar is based. It is also apposite that at its December 2017 graduation ceremony, the University of Stellenbosch honoured Prof. Aslam Fataar by awarding him the Chancellor's Medal for Excellence in Research.

A few of the essays included in this collection first appeared in the *Annual Review of Islam in South Africa* (ARISA), which is a yearly analysis of and report on important events and developments in the Muslim community and is published by the Centre for Contemporary Islam, based at the Religious Studies Department at the University of Cape Town.

I am deeply honoured to pen these few words in support of the ruminations of Prof. Aslam Fataar. I know that the readers of this book will learn much from it and that these sermons and essays will inspire passion and action in the next generation of those who speak truth to power.

Imam Dr A Rashied Omar

Imam of the Claremont Main Road Masjid, Cape Town, South Africa
Research Scholar of Islamic Studies and Peacebuilding, University of Notre Dame, Indiana, USA

20 May 2019

3. EDITOR'S FOREWORD

It is again time for "a new first" in the Beyers Naudè Centre Series on Public Theology. It came about with a request by Nico Koopman, former Director of the Centre and current Vice-Rector for Community Interaction and Personnel at Stellenbosch University, for the consideration of the publication of a collection of essays, opinion pieces and sermons from a different religious tradition. Up to now, all 12 volumes in the Series – edited editions by multiple authors as well as collected essays or monographs by individual authors – were by Christian authors. Therefore, we invited Aslam Fataar to consider sharing some of his work on public theological themes with us.

Even if the concept of public theology may not be as common in Islamic Theology or Studies as in Christian discourse, it does not mean it does not exist in Islam! In fact, in 1995, Pakistani Muslim scholar Ausaf Ali, reflecting on the development of his own interest in public theology – a term that, according to him at the time was "much less known and used in the Islamic world" and that, by then, "the two words – public and theology – joined together", he "had neither heard nor seen in print."[1] Studying Christian understandings and writings on public theology, he realised that he has always been a public theologian himself!

Ali continues by saying,

> Actually I would not even hesitate to call Moses and Jesus and Muhammad (peace be on them) public theologians; which does not detract from the fact that they were prophets. [And], [a]t any rate our *'ulamā'* (religiously learned men who speak on social, political, economic, ethical, etc., issues) are definitely public theologians as are, of course, indeed, the Jewish rabbis, Catholic priests, Protestant ministers, etc., who concern themselves with the problems of the world.[2]

With this volume in the series we therefore have the privilege to share a collection of public theological reflections written over a period of 25 years by Aslam Fataar. He is not only a respected scholar – the latter as Distinguished Professor in Education (specifically in the areas of Sociology of Education and Education Policy) at Stellenbosch University – but also a well-known South African, Muslim, public commentator. It is, thus, not surprising that theologian David Tracy's view of theology being done in three publics, namely the church (mosque), the academy and within broader society, finds expression in these works from Fataar's pen. The collection paints not only a picture of his involvement in exactly these three publics – from sermons delivered in mosques, academic papers and opinion pieces in newspapers all with public theological characteristics or implications – but, also, arranged chronologically, it offers a fascinating view of the history of our country, with the challenges it faced and still faces as well as the successes achieved or

1 Ali, A. 1995. An essay on Public Theology. *Islamic Studies* 34(1):67-89.
2 Ali, A. An essay on Public Theology, 67.

opportunities sadly missed. We trust that our readers will equally enjoy, be enriched and be challenged by this collection.

Len Hansen

Editor: Beyers Naudè Centre Series on Public Theology

1. INTRODUCTION

The chapters in this anthology were written from my perspective as an engaged Muslim activist. They speak to political and Muslim socio-cultural contexts as these unfolded during the 25-year post-apartheid period. They are my attempt to give religio-political character to this period and make a statement about the interaction between Islam, politics and ethics in Cape Town.

This anthology is comprised of sermons (*khuṭab*), newspaper articles and opinion pieces. I present them as my evolving thoughts about Islam and Muslim life in Cape Town. It should be of particular interest to high school and university students, and those interested in one person's engaged perspective from an ethical religious standpoint. The foundation for this text was laid in my political socialisation during my high school years at Parkwood High School in Ottery, and my student years at the University of the Western Cape (UWC). I was part of a generation of students who were politicised by the heroic student boycotts of 1980 and 1981, when students took control of schools across the Cape Flats to reject gutter apartheid education. We launched self-directed alternative education programmes and established a myriad of clubs and societies. I became the chairperson of the debating society at my school at 15 years old, and was the chairperson of the school chess club for three years, in addition to participating in a full range of sport activities during my school years.

Reading, arguing and experimenting with various sets of leftist ideas became the *sine qua non* of our political diet. This happened while we participated throughout the 1980s in a plethora of youth, sport, political and recreational clubs and societies. I found particular resonance for my activism through my participation in the late 1980s in the United Democratic Front (UDF) aligned Save the Press campaign where I represented *Al-Qalam*, the Muslim Youth Movement's monthly newspaper, which was banned at that time.

The year 1983 represented an inflection point that brought my early life trajectory into conversation with my ensuing Muslim religious political path. I was by this stage thoroughly politicised, yet living a life immersed in the popular culture of the time, while pursuing a youth activist path. A momentous event was my attendance of the launch of the UDF in Rocklands in August 1983. I finished writing Matric in that year as a 17-year-old and started in December to do casual sales work selling clothing at Lightbody's Clothing Store in downtown Claremont. While working there, I attended Friday congregational prayers at the Al-Jaamia Mosque in Stegmann Road, where the charismatic Imam Ebrahim 'Sep' Davids (1936-1998) officiated. Imam Sep, as he was fondly known, was erudite and outspoken. He delivered his sermons in English, which I found attractive and beguiling despite my limited ability in the language. Like the majority of kids from the Cape Flats, my mother tongue is Kaaps Afrikaans. Imam Sep followed in the footsteps of Imam Abdullah Haron as the Imam of the Al-Jaamia Mosque.

It was in this context that I was introduced to the figure of Imam Haron, the renowned revolutionary Muslim leader who was martyred by the apartheid regime in September 1969. The logical development of the book culminates in a set of four chapters that draw on Imam Abdullah Haron's legacy. It is no coincidence that this martyrological figure has emerged so powerfully in the last two years. We are in the midst of commemorating the fiftieth anniversary of his martyrdom. Together with all other martyrs killed by the apartheid machinery, his death has given generations of people the capacity to imagine life. The chapters on Imam Haron call attention to the necessity of living an ethical life, in the service of others, and I make a call in the book for mobilising the Imam's ethical commitments in the newer terrain of the twenty-first century with vastly different circumstances and challenges, one of the most important of which is the threat associated with climate change and global warming, a theme that I focus on in two of the book's later chapters.

The question that we have to turn to in contemporary times is how we use the ethical figure of the martyr to respond to what has been described as the 'post-human' condition in respect of which humans, machines and technology are now merging in novel and unpredictable ways to provide the substantive outlines of our lives. Answering this question will require new conceptual frames based on courageous and novel readings of texts and contexts. This is the stuff of exciting, yet urgent, intellectual work during the next months and years.

It was out of the Al-Jaamia Mosque context that I began to experiment autodidactically with a kind of engaged, yet somewhat independent-minded, activist persona. This is the discursive environment that sparked the orientation towards independent thinking that has been a feature of my adult life. My activist life was always an uneasy balance between positive, engaged participation, on the one hand, and the struggle to stand back and develop an independent, even detached, eye on political developments, on the other. I felt that the anti-apartheid moment required diligent, committed participation more than the armchair critic's equivocation. However, while activism always won out in the end, a cautious attitude towards political dogma lodged itself in my being, which influenced how I organised the thoughts that I express in the various chapters of this text.

It was at a different mosque, not more than five hundred meters away from the Al-Jaamia, Stegmann Road mosque, where I, together with a number of my Muslim youth activist comrades, became inspired by another revolutionary Imam, the redoubtable Imam Hassan Solomon (1941-2009), who was then officiating at the Claremont Main Road Mosque (CMRM). This mosque would become my and my family's resident mosque. I came across Imam Hassan when I decided one Friday to attend his *jumuʿah* congregational service. I remembered that he spoke at the UDF launch rally, but hearing him speak from the *mimbar* (pulpit) was a galvanising moment. Erudite, passionate and rousing, his sermons were infused with anti-apartheid rhetoric delivered in the language of Islam. He presented a critique of apartheid and passionately argued for racial equality, fairness and democracy in an Islamic idiom.

Imam Hassan was for me the first Imam to make an explicit connection between Islam and racial justice. This simple, yet profound connection ran counter to the lack of political content that was the staple at the majority of mosques in the city. The Muslim leadership in the city had practised a type of acquiescence, some even say an accepting attitude, in response to apartheid repression. Mainstream Muslim discourses were by and large ceremonial and inward looking. Imam Hassan was an example of the younger generation of students and professionals who began to develop a type of political Islam that attempted to mobilise people to take up an anti-apartheid stance.

Imam Hassan's political Islamic discourses provided us with the motivation and energy to tie our leftist protest commitments to an Islamic language. While still in autodidactic mode, we began experimenting with our own readings of religious texts, including reading the Qur'an, and a range of books on Islam written in English that found their way to Cape Town. Voracious reading was key to experimenting with anti-apartheid politics from an Islamic perspective. We were fashioning our youthful activist identity via a set of novel conceptual repertoires based on reading and mapping Islamic concepts onto debates associated with the anti-apartheid struggle addressing questions such as social justice, human rights and gender equality. Many of these themes run through the chapters in this text.

This approach accompanied me through my student years at UWC and my years of teaching at Parkwood High School, since renamed Lotus High School, where I returned in 1988 to teach. UWC was a key venue for my intellectual becoming, first as an undergraduate, then part-time graduate student during the 1980s and 1990s, and then as academic from the mid-1990s. I practised my activist politics while participating in a range of educational, youth, religious, sport and civic organisations, often as a project leader of sorts or member of the leadership of these organisations. These were exhilarating times for young adults. We had loads of energy and clarity of purpose that galvanised our anti-apartheid politics. As the 1990s stretched into the 2000s and beyond, this clarity was reoriented to deal with the realpolitik and complexities associated with democratic governance, unmet expectations and the faltering nature of the emerging post-apartheid state.

As my personal political path began to merge with my academic becoming, eventually being dominated by my immersion in academia and the need to conform to the professional expectations of academic work, I managed to sustain a Muslim public commitment through my work as a consultant editor of the *Al-Qalam* newspaper, teaching an Islamic Studies class at the CMRM Saturday *madrasa,* periodic appearances on various radio programmes on Islamic radio, and in later years as a board member of the International Peace College South Africa (IPSA). I also did some research work on the sociology of Muslim education, aspects of which appear in various chapters of this collection. CMRM remained a ubiquitous presence as a venue for the expression of my voice as an engaged Muslim.

While my first association with the mosque was through exposure to Imam Hassan Solomon's sermons in the 1984/5 period, it was, however, under the leadership of Imam Rashied Omar, who became the Imam of the mosque in 1986, that the mosque became the key venue in South Africa for practising and conceptually elaborating progressive Islamic commitments in the context of the struggle against apartheid and as an exemplary and courageous vehicle for a socially just expression of Islam. The mosque established institutional infrastructure and an accompanying Islamic progressive language under Imam Rashied's leadership. This was informed by pluralistic and human rights commitments in the unfolding democratic terrain, and a robust social justice platform from where the mosque exercises its Islamic commitments to the poor, needy and socially marginalised communities of

Cape Town. These commitments are exemplified by its various development projects in a number of communities across the city.

I became a mosque congregant by way of the mosque's informal links with the Muslim Students Association (MSA) and the Muslim Youth Movement of South Africa (MYMSA), to which I belonged. The latter two organisations had an active organisational presence in the Western Cape, with branches in many suburbs and townships. While serving as the mosque's Imam, Rashied Omar was also the national president of the MYMSA until he left the latter position in 1989. Led by Omar and its national director, Mawlānā Ebrahim Moosa, the MYMSA entered a period of what was labelled as the search for 'Islamic localisation' or 'contextualism'. I joined the MYMSA in 1987, eventually becoming its national Deputy President in 1991. The MYMSA grappled intensively with the need to move away from Islamist frames imported from the Muslim heartlands, especially from the Muslim Brotherhood in Egypt and the Jamā`at-i-Islāmī in Pakistan.

I experienced this contextualisation experiment as exhilarating, especially the many arguments that some of us had with the MYM old guard, who remained committed to the notion of an 'Islamic Movement'. This latter perspective can be summed up as a type of idealistic commitment to normative Islam based on the ideals of striving for the perfect Islamic society. In practice, the Islamic Movement perspective too easily translated into a political stance that prevented the MYMSA from taking up an active anti-apartheid role. As a newbie in the MYMSA, not tied to the idea of an Islamic Movement, I participated in the search for a local and relevant Islamic discourse tied to a commitment to democracy and human rights.

This was the period when the MYMSA advanced an Islamic discourse in respect of anti-racism, gender equality, religious pluralism and productive co-existence in a secular democracy. We began to read a range of texts other than the usual Islamic Movement type of books written by authors such as Abū-l`Alā Mawdūdī, (1903-1979) Sayyid Sābiq (1915-2000), Yūsuf al-Qaraḍāwī (1926), and Sayyid Quṭb (1906-1966). The MYMSA members in Cape Town began to read texts that concentrated on Islam and its application in modern contexts. I, for example, attended and later coordinated a set of critical reading groups where we read texts by Islamic scholars such as Fazlur Raḥmān (1919-1988), Mohamed Arkoun (1928-2010) and Fāṭima Mernissi (1940-2015). I fondly remember reading and discussing a set of three books by Fazlur Raḥmān in Saturday afternoon tutorial sessions. Led by Ebrahim Moosa, these sessions were free-wheeling and dialogical as we endeavoured to create a safe, yet challenging, pedagogical space. We questioned and criticised freely, read the texts carefully, and developed theoretical tools to help us work out how to pursue a generative reading of the Islamic scriptures in the light of modern and everyday local challenges.

While we have moved on from the modernist frames of Fazlur Raḥmān, his intellectual methodology of interpreting the Qur'ān and other sources in the light of contemporary circumstances (see Raḥmān 1982) stayed with me. And while we adopted what has been called 'critical traditional' Islamic lenses that emphasise methodical historicised readings of the entire Islamic legacy and its application through rigorous social scientifically inspired understandings of the contemporary world, I still dip into some of Raḥmān's texts to refresh and reinvigorate my own interpretive methodological approaches. Raḥmān's emphasis on novel contextual readings of the Qur'an was formative and his influence on me in this regard is apparent in this book, especially its responsiveness to local contextual challenges.

My commitment to a contextual reading, as exemplified in this text, can be said to be an outflow of my intellectual socialisation in the MYMSA's experiment from the mid-1980s with 'contextual Islam', its rehearsal in the intellectually engaged space of the Claremont Main Road Mosque, and reading scholarly Islamic texts that provided me with a methodology to substantively develop a socially relevant Islamic discourse. It is no coincidence that half of the chapters in this book are sermons delivered at the mosque. In one way or the other, our attempt to tie Islam to democracy, pluralism and justice informs all the chapters in the book.

The chapters in the anthology are organised in chronological order. The first chapter is a *khuṭbah* that I delivered at CMRM in 1994 and the final chapter is one delivered at the mosque on 31 May, Ramaḍān, 2019. As indicated earlier, the first chapters are based on a somewhat optimistic reading of the political imperative and the need for Muslims to actively participate in the post-apartheid development of the country. The book can thus be regarded as nation-state-centric; in other words, it proffers the nation as the basis for its cultural and religious reflections. It stands to reason that our apartheid-devastated country would require a serious national programme to rebuild its governmental infrastructure and provide houses, hospitals and schools. The activist stance that I favoured is to contribute to this project, and it is this nation-building vision that animates my activist-intellectual orientation in this book.

This optimistic nation-building perspective is attenuated by the end of the book. Socio-economic decline, faltering governmental infrastructure and systemic collapse were exacerbated by widespread state corruption during the last ten years. Governmental politics were 'overdetermined' by the politics of the belly. State capture became the dominant raison d'être, compromising governmental capacity to build a functional developmental state. The last ten wasted years spawned corrosive dynamics in the body politic. The majority of the country's citizens foundered in a context where basic service delivery became neglected, which left them exposed to unremittingly harsh living conditions.

From around 2009 a series of chapters in the book offers a critique of governmental politics and Muslims' adherence to an easy accommodation and support of the ruling party. It makes a plea for the Muslim leadership and civic organisations to develop a critical distance from the ruling government, at times to offer constructive critique when required, and at other times denounce and call out the government and ruling party on its corruption and anti-poor policies. I argued that the qur'anic requirement of bearing witness to injustice, of calling out corruption and state infrastructural collapse made it necessary for Muslim civil society to develop a critical distance from government. Alignment with broader civic social justice struggles in support of pro-poor development would be the preferred ethical path. Cosying up to the ruling party would compromise Muslims and other communities in walking such a path.

Regarding the emerging socio-cultural landscape after the first elections in 1994, the book turns its attention very early to at least two dimensions that emerged quickly and dramatically on the democratic landscape: the first is the complex socio-economic landscape and Muslims' adaptations to this landscape, and the second is the rapid impact of global flows on local Muslims' discursive orientations. The first aspect refers to the complex and diverse social and educational landscape that emerged after 1994. The book, for example, offers a number of chapters on Muslim educational patterns in Cape Town. The aim here was to develop a descriptive language that would help the community engage with the educational spaces and circumstances in which children now accomplish their schooling. These chapters point to a range of cultural and identification adaptations that Muslim communities have been making to secure quality schooling. The larger purpose of this theme is to illuminate the complexities involved in living in a post-apartheid city generally, and the specific manifestation of these newer realities for Muslims in their endeavours to establish worthwhile lives. A key dimension of this situation is the increasing poverty experienced by people, including Muslims. While the growing middle class has accessed wealth through the opening up of greater educational and professional opportunities, the chasm between rich and poor has widened, and impoverished livelihoods are the majority experience in the city. Tying one's communal and religious commitments to the systemic alleviation of poverty and hardship is presented in the book as a core ethical and social justice priority.

The second aspect refers to the diversification of local Muslim discourses through the global Muslim networks and influences that flowed into the city after the end of apartheid. Transnational flows of ideas and meanings by way of Muslim refugees and migrants from Africa and the rest of the world, accompanied by information technological connectivity, enriched the Sufi mystical scene. A greater range of credal expressions associated with maximalist and austere readings of Islam also found popular resonance in the city and country. This enriched and broadened the diversity of Islamic expressions, while at the same time eliciting anxieties that translated, for example, into expressions of vigilante forms of protection to respond to the upsurge in drugs and crime. I particularly address this anxiety in two chapters written in the early 2000s in which I invoke the historical Islamicate figure of Abū Jahl, an inveterate opponent of the Prophet Muhammad (peace be upon him), to point to the unproductiveness of violence-prone articulations of grievances to deal with complex social problems.

The increasingly heterodox expression of Islamic discourses also led to periodic skirmishes which threatened Muslims' communal cohesion. The Salafi-Sufi clashes of the early 2000s were a local inflection with latent roots in Cape Muslim history. Proponents of a purist, austere brand of (Salafi) Islam hit out at the increase in mystical (Sufi) Muslim trends, whose growth was spurred by an infusion of 'spiritual energy' supplied by various transnational networks that found a home in Cape Town. And the Shi`a community's growth in some cities in South Africa initially led to low-level recriminations and culminated in a fatal attack by an unknown group on a Shi`a mosque in Verulam, Durban in May 2018. In a chapter in the book that was written after the attack I call on Muslims to join attempts to take decisive action in order to stymy sectarian tendencies in the community, and for them to properly embrace intra-religious pluralism and dialogue as a means of establishing social cohesion through concerted concentration on social justice issues in the community.

This book is an attempt to define and occupy the middle ground and build a conversational space that would avoid framing the community as adversarial and lacking a shared language. The book attempts to impel an inclusive dialogue and to create common ground. Generating such common ground would afford the community a space to begin to figure out how discourses enter into, and play out, in our everyday lives and regulate our behaviour. Understanding some of these tropes will provide a basis to more adequately respond to the challenges that confront the community. Commitment to justice, openness, intra-religious tolerance, and developing complex Islamic literacies are essential. The urgency of developing spaces of engagement and deliberation is unquestionable. Walking a dialogical path to build social spaces and institutions of engagement will be tough and even appear to be counter-intuitive to some. This book is a call for the careful and deliberative generation of dialogical spaces, especially in the myriad Muslim educational institutions that have emerged in the country since 1994, for nurturing respectful and inclusive dialogue across historically ossified boundaries. It is only through building a society on the basis of the qur'anic imperative of mutual and inclusive dialogue and engagement that Muslims in our beloved country would be able to secure our future and contribute to the future of fellow citizens.

REFERENCES

Raḥmān, F. 1982. *Islam and Modernity: Transformations of an Intellectual Tradition.* London, University of Chicago Press.

Said, E. 2000. *Representations of the Intellectual.* New York, Vintage Books.

2. ACTIVE PARTICIPATION IN THE RECONSTRUCTION AND DEVELOPMENT PROGRAMME[1]

This *khuṭbah* aims at provoking debate on the imperative of active participation by Muslims in the development of South Africa. It specifically considers a framework for participation, and makes concrete proposals for active Muslim involvement.

It attempts to answer the vexing question: How do ordinary Muslims become involved in the reconstruction and development of an apartheid-ravaged South Africa in which the overwhelming majority of people live in inhuman conditions?

During the dark years of apartheid many sectors of society, including some Muslim organisations, vigorously opposed the injustice and oppression of the apartheid state. Organisations such as the Call of Islam, Muslim Youth Movement, Qibla and the Muslim Students Association actively organised against state policies. These organisations and others were giving concrete expression to the principle of establishing justice as they are exhorted to do in the Qur'an:

> *O you who believe, Stand out firmly for justice as witness-bearers to Allah* (Q. 4:V135)

Thus, the epitome of 'striving for justice' during the apartheid era was the expression of opposition to apartheid and to demand the establishment of a democratic and legitimate state. To be concerned with justice meant to oppose apartheid. One could say that the logical possibilities of our actions were limited to fervent and passionate opposition, for which some were persecuted and incarcerated in prison.

Today in a post-apartheid South Africa, having accomplished political democracy, 'standing out firmly for justice' has come to acquire a different shade of meaning. In the pursuit of the goal of socio-economic justice – an ideal which Islam shares with other freedom-loving people – the challenge is to move from oppositional modes of action to a development mode.

Muslims, like the rest of society, are now confronted with the more difficult task of socio-economic reconstruction. The supply of housing, health care and sanitation presents enormous challenges of delivery to the democratic state. This process will require the active participation of all sectors of society including Muslims.

Muslim participation (or non-participation) is part of the broader issue about what type of citizens we want to be. Many still see themselves as Indian or Malay, or as belonging to some other ethnic group. We are struggling to imbibe attitudes reflective of people living in and committed to black African South Africa. The reluctance by some to see ourselves as South African citizens prevents us from adopting attitudes that will facilitate commitment to our country and full participation in its development.

---

1 *Khuṭbah* delivered at CMRM, published in a mosque-issued booklet titled, *The role of Muslims in the RDP*, 1994.

We have, in some respects, misappropriated and overplayed our apparent Malaysian, Indonesian or Indian connections. Instead of using Malaysia's example of development and affirmative inclusivity for the benefit of all South Africans, we choose to use the ethicised connection to enhance a specific 'ethnic' identity, which places Muslims in isolation from others. The same applies to some Muslims' use of their Indian ethnic origins to set themselves apart from others. This runs contrary to the principles of non-racialism and nation-building in the post-apartheid era.

The example of reconstruction and development in Malaysia should inspire us, not our imagined ethnic connection to the country, as some have done recently. This can only occur if we speak about Malaysia's affirmative action experiences and its stable economic environment, which is based on creativity and a healthy relationship between labour, capital and the state.

The economic success of Malaysia is based on low profit margins, reasonable wages, consensual development priorities and technological capability. Their pluralistic political system is human-rights friendly and is based on consensus-building. These are the qualities and elements that our (tenuous) Malaysian connection should highlight as this would aid reconstruction and development for the benefit of all.

The basis of Muslim participation is provided by the dynamic institution of *zakāh* (wealth-sharing). Allah (SWT) declares in the Qur'an in *Sūrah* (Chapter) *al-Ḥajj* (The pilgrimage);

> *(They are) those who, if we establish them in the land, they establish regular prayer and give regular charity (zakāh), enjoin the right and forbid the wrong. With Allah rests the end of all affairs.* (Q. 22:V41)

In the words of Sayyid Sābiq in his book *Zakāh: The Third Pillar* (1994), "*zakāh* is the pivotal institution for national development and providing for the social welfare needs of the community".

Sābiq mentions the category of *māl al-birr* – giving of one's wealth (other than the obligatory *Zakāh*) – as an act of righteousness – to indicate the necessity of funding development.

The problem with our expression of *zakāh* is that we have collapsed it into a welfare focus. A challenge for our *zakāh* institutions is to insert the development dimension in such a manner that it could contribute to the RDP. Also, the polemics around whether *zakāh* can be given to non-Muslims has prevented us from responding positively to the demands of the masses. The time has come to resolve these and other problems that might impede our participation in the RDP.

Proposals for Muslim participation in the RDP

1. Individuals could participate at a community level in the local civics and various projects such as relief work, primary health care, library groups and educational projects.
2. We could make available our institutions such as *masājid* (mosques) and *madāris* (religious schools) to meet the social welfare needs of the entire community. Why, for example, can a medical clinic staffed by volunteers not be attached to a *masjid*?

3. Youths could become involved in youth development through the Western Cape Youth Forum and the Regional Youth Development Committee. These bodies focus on youth development in under-resourced and deprived areas.

4. Muslims have been blessed with expertise in various fields. This expertise could be made available to development projects.

5. We should incorporate into our madrasa syllabus a component on social studies to engender in our children an empathetic approach to the needy and poor.

6. The development of an appropriate investment ethic should be generated. If we argue that International Monetary Fund (IMF) and World Bank-sponsored loans and international aid will impact negatively on change, then we would have to come up with alternative financial strategies. Muslim businessmen would have to consider investing in empowerment and development, and funding of prospective black entrepreneurs. We need to loosen up the concentration of money within Muslim circles.

7. And finally, mosques could consider how, as institutions, they can contribute to the RDP. An RDP fund, financed by congregants, could possibly be administered from the *Masjid*.

In conclusion, the *khuṭbah* emphasises that Islam prescribes active participation in establishing justice and proscribes passivity. Participation in reconstruction and development for the benefit of all South Africans, in terms of the arguments outlined in this *khuṭbah,* is a highly commendable act. This is emphasised and corroborated by Allah (SWT) in *Ṣūrah al-Nisā* (The women);

> *Not equal are those Believers who sit (at home) and receive no hurt, And those who strive and fight in the path of God with their goods and their persons ...* (Q. 4:V95)

REFERENCE

Sābiq, S. 1994. *Zakāh, the Third Pillar.* (Translated by Yusuf da Costa). Durban, Muslim Youth Movement of South Africa.

3. MUSLIM SCHOOLING PATTERNS IN THE NEW SOUTH AFRICA[1]

Demographic profiles in the South African schooling system have been changing rapidly over the last few years subsequent to the deracialisation of public life. New patterns of school interaction have been established. While the quest for quality education has undergirded these new patterns, factors such as the preservation of community identity have also played a role. Moreover, community schooling patterns are developing in the context of fragile nation-building processes.

This chapter focuses on schooling patterns that have emerged in the Muslim community over the last few years. Contrary to the popular perception of Muslims as an undifferentiated mass, their schooling patterns show a diversity of interactions with the education system. The basis of the Muslim community's diverse interactions with schooling is determined by an interplay of a number of elements, which include race, class, identity and prior educational patterns. These interactions have taken place against the backdrop of the larger canvas of educational reform over the last few years in South Africa.

NATIONAL EDUCATIONAL REFORM

Schooling patterns that have emerged recently are directly related to the educational policy environment put in place by the state. Education policy has thus far been ambivalent about the two contesting aims of equity and growth. On the one hand, the state has shown a commitment to eradicating educational inequality through its insistence on an equity-driven policy environment. One the other hand, the achievement of equity is constrained by the cautionary discourse of economic growth, a position that holds that nations such as South Africa ought to cut their education budgets if they want to grow and become part of the global political economy. Thus, policy ambivalence has manifested because of the equalisation of education taking place within the limits of a financially austere budgetary framework.

A number of reform policies have been adopted and are now being enacted. These policies have been constructing – and in many cases entrenching – a public schooling system which provides the backdrop for community interaction. The Schools Act adopted in 1996 (Department of Education 1996) is the most important piece of legislation currently determining school attendance patterns.

It permits a financial arrangement in which parental fees play a crucial role in the quality of schooling and this has led to the entrenchment of a dual schooling pattern.

Middle-class parents who can afford to pay fees are opting to send their children to former white schools in search of quality education. The children of working-class parents who are unable to contribute to schools financially continue to attend low-quality schools in their neighbourhoods. Ironically, the teacher rationalisation

1 Published in *Annual Review of Islam in South Africa*, Centre for Contemporary Islam, UCT, 1998, Vol. 1.

process, which purported to be aimed at achieving equity across the system, had led to the further deterioration of schooling in the 'coloured' areas of the Western Cape.

A minority of South African children acquire an internationally competitive quality education, which guarantees exposure to a sophisticated curriculum that will enable them to work in the service and information industries. Working-class children, by contrast, are exposed to low-quality education in which the allure of youth subcultures is often more powerful than the school. It is in this context that community schools, such as the recently established Muslim schools on the Cape Flats, attempt to engender a qualitative educational culture by employing an identity discourse to counter the perceived 'moral corruption' that characterises township life.

MUSLIMS AND THE MODEL C EXPERIENCE

Muslim attendance at former Model C white schools has increased exponentially over the last five years and particularly after the 1994 election. While some of these children now live in the former white neighbourhoods in which these schools are located, most Muslim children travel more than five kilometres to attend these schools. They come from lower-middle-class and middle-class families who are able to afford the school fees and travelling costs necessary to gain access. These families realise the value of quality education in positioning their children advantageously for later life.

Muslim children at these schools come under enormous pressure to assimilate into the dominant liberal culture. They are exposed to the Eurocentric cultural world of their white counterparts. While multi-cultural in orientation, offering multi-faith religious education, for example, their curriculum supports secular values and is disposed towards engendering a liberal detachment from developmental concerns.

Muslim children, together with other black children at these schools, also suffer subtle forms of racism. In such an environment, they have difficulty in finding acceptability as full members of the dominant school culture. Moreover, their attendance at these schools results in alienation from their own cultural world. This double alienation has profound implications for issues of identity.

However, Muslim children at Model C schools are not simply victims of the hegemonic liberal culture. They are showing tenacity in the way they confront the homogenising culture of the schools. One example is offered by Muslim boys at one of the Cape's top Southern Suburbs boys' schools who formed themselves into a protection unit after being physically attacked by white boys at the school. Collectively they come to the aid of individuals who are attacked and they target the perpetrators for physical retribution. In an interview with me they used concepts such as "*jihād*" (personal struggle), "*qiṭāl*" (fighting) and "*ummah*" (community of the faithful) to justify taking action to protect their right to be at the school and to command respect.

The establishment of Muslim Student Associations (MSAs) at Model C schools is another example of Muslim students' resistance to cultural domination. Historically, MSAs operated in coloured and Indian schools during the 1970s and 1980s. They supported a non-racial discourse in their opposition to apartheid. The MSAs at

Model C schools, however, were established as a means for nurturing religious identity and as an organisational vehicle for empowering Muslim students to interact with the dominant culture at their schools. The MSA provides students with a sense of place and significance under circumstances in which they are at risk of being usurped culturally. Muslim students have been able, through the MSA, to lay claim to recognition and respect that they might have struggled to claim as individuals. Thus, while they were able to access Model C schools that secured them quality education, such access also exposed them to a complex cultural context. Muslims and other black children are victims of daily cultural and racial insensitivity, which prevents them from becoming part of the dominant cultural identity. However, Muslim students have shown a willingness to engage this domination by appropriating their own religious symbols, which allows them to stake a claim to equal recognition and worth in Model C schools.

THE RISE OF MUSLIM COMMUNITY SCHOOLS ON THE CAPE FLATS

Three Muslim high schools have been established on the Cape Flats over the last five years. A fourth school, a primary school, was established by means of a partnership between Egypt's al-Azhar University and the Muslim Judicial Council, the main theological body in the Western Cape. These schools are funded through a combination of parental fees (a nominal amount), community fund-raising and donor money from the business sector. The schools were established with the primary aim of providing an Islam-centred religious and moral education. They follow the core state curriculum and are registered with the Western Cape Education Department. They provide ancillary subjects in Islamic Studies, Arabic and Islamic law (*fiqh*).

The location of the schools on the Cape Flats is indicative of their broader purpose and social function. They are found in largely working- and lower-middle-class environments, where a perception of the diminished worth of public schooling is becoming widespread. The public schools in the township are perceived to suffer from what has nebulously been termed a 'lack of a culture of learning'. Youth subcultures, influenced by a violent gang underworld and the general instability of township life, have a detrimental effect on the functioning of such schools. A real and perceived collapse of morality amongst young people has become a perpetual lament from religious structures. The Muslim community school stepped into this breach with the promise of a morally sound educational programme based on strong religious principles.

Parents send their children to these schools to give them access to an education that is intended to generate moral and religious propriety. Parents hope that this will act as a bulwark against the corrupting culture that is pervasive in township life. However, these children are caught between the moral culture of the Muslim community school and the prevailing norms of their townships. They often flit between two identities: the narrow one of the school during school hours and a less constrained leisure identity over the weekend. While some do this skilfully, most children are not adept at marshalling a coherent identity to govern their school and extracurricular lives. The success of Muslim community schools will depend on their willingness and ability to provide a framework for adaptation in terms of which their students can develop a coherent identity to function with moral propriety and flexibility in township life.

MUSLIM MISSION PRIMARY SCHOOLS

The first mission primary school in Cape Town was established in 1913. Although these schools receive a state grant that pays for their teachers' wages, all of them were built and are sustained by the community. All consumable items are paid for by community fundraising. They follow a state syllabus and provide basic Islamic Studies.

They were established in the first half of the twentieth century as counterparts to the Christian missionary schools that sprang up in coloured areas. As Cape Muslims' first contact with formal schooling, Muslim primary schools served as an instrument of modernisation and adaptation to a changing Cape Town. These schools are different from the Muslim community schools, discussed in the previous section, in that they have always been firmly located in the mainstream bureaucratic structures of government.

They are attracting many children from the surrounding working-class neighbourhoods and many students are transported to them daily from all over the Cape Flats. As in the case of Muslim community high schools, parents send their children to these schools in a quest for a religious and moral education. Parents also tap into a rich Cape Muslim identity and sense of community cultivated by these schools over a few decades. They have a moral culture that is much less stringent but no less visible than at the community high schools, enabling their students to relate more coherently to their extracurricular cultural world.

However, these schools have come under pressure to improve their quality in the face of competition from Model C schools, to which they have lost many of their best students. Moreover, the teaching culture is under the same threat of erosion that other public schools are experiencing. The teacher cutbacks and multiple layers of educational change in ill-prepared contexts have a disorientating effect on school learning programmes.

These schools face the challenge of improving their educational quality and so affording an equitable learning experience for their students. While their problems are not dissimilar to those of other working-class schools, they have a supportive community and alumni. If properly mobilised, financial and infrastructural support from these sources would enable Muslim primary schools to flourish in the new context.

CONCLUSION

Muslim patterns of schooling show a diversity which belies their popular image of homogeneity. The different Muslim responses are the result of an interplay of racial, class, cultural and historical forces, which are mediated in a material reality. The common denominator is the role played by religious and cultural considerations in shaping Muslim responses and interactions. Lack of space has not allowed this chapter to focus on the schooling experiences of Muslim children who attend working-class secular schools or the many "cram colleges" that have sprung up in Cape Town.

4. BREAKING FROM ABŪ JAHL'S SHADOW: SOUTH AFRICAN MUSLIMS' SEARCH FOR A 'THEOLOGY OF SOFTNESS'[1]

South African Muslims are currently affected by very crucial adaptation processes. This is illustrated by our response to the Palestinian crisis, certain Muslims' reaction to the proposed anti-terror laws, and our attitudes to accusations of complicity in the recent bombings in Cape Town. We have sent mixed signals about our willingness to develop an identity that connects with, and is part of, a broader productive South Africanness.

Often the most audible Muslim responses are produced by those we hear in the media and on public platforms, but not necessarily from the silent majority. These responses reflect an ambivalent narrow identity that is disconnected from broader social processes. Muslim isolationism, I believe, is at its root driven by the urge to invent relatively comfortable lifestyles in a 'sea of chaos' caused by the disruptive impact of social transformation.

Our current religious and theological discourses are informed by a stance that prevents us from interacting productively with our social context. Words of anger and hostility come from many community leaders. Verbal posturing can often be heard on some of our radios and *manābir* (pulpits). The world is presented in stark, almost conspiratorial terms. This discourse is intensified in crisis periods when the heat is turned up, producing a siege mentality. Most Muslims maintain a kind of antagonistic lack of interest.

ABŪ JAHL'S TRAGIC MISRECOGNITION

Reflecting on the iconic figure of Amr bin Ḥishām, more famously known as Abū Jahl (father of the ignorant), allows us to understand how a community or individuals can get trapped by their words and actions. Abū Jahl features strongly in the *sīrah* (historical accounts of Prophet Muhammad's life - peace be upon him). Abū Jahl represented the views of all those in Makkah who opposed the Prophet's message of *tawḥīd* (God's unicity) and social justice. The message of Islam came to threaten the social organisation of hierarchy, power and privilege of pre-Islamic Makkah.

During the early years of the Islamic community in Makkah, Abū Jahl conspired to hound out and persecute the Prophet. Negotiating the social and tribal hierarchy of Makkan society, Abū Jahl tried various ways to isolate the Prophet, but without success. The Prophet, enjoying the protection of his uncle Abū Ṭālib, through the latter's elevated tribal status, forged ahead with his mission with fortitude and commitment. Desperate, Abū Jahl even tried to kill the Prophet, but he was unsuccessful.

1 CMRM *khuṭbah*, published in *Al-Qalam*, December 2000.

What is remarkable about Abū Jahl's story is that despite his vehemence against the Prophet's work, he also recognised the veracity of the Prophet's mission. But his recognition was partial. Biographers of the Prophet note that on at least three occasions, under cover of darkness. Abū Jahl was caught outside the Prophet's house listening to the latter reciting passages from the Qur'an. He was overcome by the persuasiveness of their logic.

Abū Jahl's recognition was partial because he could not take the next step, that is, to make the necessary psycho-social adjustments, which would involve cultivating a fundamentally new orientation and outlook, become Muslim, and consequently join the fight against the power elites of Makkah. Tragically, Abū Jahl was compromised by his anti-Prophet words and rhetoric. Over many years he became a master in vilifying the Prophet, arousing passions and spreading an atmosphere of high tension. He acquired an identity and a reputation as a rabble-rouser, an identity that precluded him from cultivating the skills to make a fundamental conceptual switch into a different, empowering and just life world. Abū Jahl was a victim of his own words and actions. Alas, he died an enemy of Islam at the battle of Badr.

ESCAPING FROM ABŪ JAHL'S SHADOW

I want to venture that, like Abū Jahl, we Muslims in South Africa may also suffer from an inability to recognise the complexity of our community-in-making processes. Instead, we remain at the level of verbal discourse, embroiled in peripheral issues, responding to and connecting with social issues only at the level of surface appearances, never able to move beyond the superficial or symptomatic. We might struggle to ask deeper questions, trapped by our words and deeds in a counter-productive logic. This has negated our ability to develop a constructive praxis that connects self and community to broader social purposes.

This truncated discourse, furthermore, prevents the community from engaging critically and in a mature way with the surrounding complexities. Here one could quite accurately speak about an entrapped theology, i.e. a religious response that is trapped in anger and verbal posturing. The community is held to ransom by having to view life through black/white frames. Think here about the antinomies of our public discourse: we speak of Islam / *kufr* (unbelief), *ḥaq* (truth) / *bāṭil* (falsehood), and *munkar* (evil) / *maʿrūf* (good). This reveals an either/or approach. The grey areas in between – where life's complexities really play out – are never given any conceptual weight. Those who do not conform are positioned as the 'evil other' at the extreme end of the theological spectrum.

Our religious language fails to provide a space for productive co-existence or the conceptual skills to deal with our interlocking identities. The fact is that we are constructed daily in and by a broad range of identity influences. As a community in flux, exposed to an open society, engulfed by the Aids pandemic, overtaken by nagging consumerism, we are in need of relating our religious lives coherently to the challenges that our varied daily relationships and interaction throw up. Alas! Our theological approach misrecognises the complications brought on by living in a complex world.

Many Muslims, recognising the limitations of this religious language as presented by the verbal controllers of '*dīn*', under the cover of darkness, almost like Abū Jahl, unexposed and under cover, find other ways and resources to deal with this complexity. They step outside of the limiting theological parameters and find solace and conceptual resources elsewhere.

More tragically, many young people, as a means of coping with the void, experiment with alternative consumer-driven lifestyles that thrive on images and cosmetic significations. They experiment with 'designer drugs', strive for an elusive yuppie lifestyle, and connect to people for whom competitiveness and individual achievement have become an all-conquering illusion. They fail to realise that the acquisitive spirit is never fulfilled, based as it is on an insatiable quest to obtain ever more and better material status.

THE UPSURGE IN POPULAR SUFISM

The current upsurge in popular Sufism (mysticism) in the Cape is an indication of the search for meaning and something tangible to mediate what is perceived as a confusing and harsh world without any fixedness. Sufism has throughout the history of Islam provided a galvanising function whenever Muslim communities have found themselves in crisis. It has become a social organiser in the absence of a unifying and direction-giving ethic.

Sufism operates as a kind of deficit mode, standing in for the absence of moral leadership and providing firm grounding in a context of great moral confusion. Sufism provides comfort and a sense of concrete attachment. Simple acts of remembering Allah provide people with a sense of certainty. This resonates with a human being's natural yearning for belonging, recognition and acknowledgment.

I do not share the rationalistically-minded person's dismissive attitude to Sufism. But I do acknowledge that Sufism can easily serve to dupe, as a palliative, to soothe the pain, while never addressing the core of the community's crisis.

Sufism has to be challenged to move people beyond a dependence on the "Master" to personal and individual empowerment so that human beings can make autonomous and responsible decisions about how they relate to and interact with the world. Here we find an inherent tension in Sufism: that is, dependence on the Master Shaykh, on the one hand, and individual autonomy, on the other; this has been depicted as a relationship of mutual antagonism, with the one necessarily excluding the other.

We watch the direction of Sufism (participating in it) in order to understand whether the relationship between autonomy and dependence can be resolved in the interests of finding our proper place in this country.

TOWARDS A THEOLOGY OF SOFTNESS

The task of developing what I term 'a theology of softness' is urgent. Here I am referring to developing an understanding of our religious resources that would enable engagement with social complexity. We are not one-dimensional beings, not just consumers or workers or producers. We are multidimensional and multifaceted beings. We interact daily with information technology and with many different types of people. We are either bosses or workers or self-employed. Many are unemployed. The angry verbal language characterising our religious discourse has prevented us from acquiring the skills and competencies to engage with the myriad relationships we transact in our daily lives.

Our theology should provide the resources to deal coherently with our complex social world. Softness refers to an attitude of respect and wisdom in dealing with the social world, taking us beyond anger, labelling, stereotyping and negative resistance – and finding productive means to engage our limitations and transcend them for the greater common good.

We have to understand how a negative verbal discourse creates 'pictures in our heads', beyond which we cannot imagine a new, more productive form of existence. South African Muslims are captivated, and held to ransom, by such mental pictures. Currently, our religious discourses concentrate only on the elucidation of these pictures, without digging beneath the images and symbols which they reflect.

A theology of softness should be aimed at moving beyond our limited frames to dealing with the complex underpinnings of our everyday life. More importantly, it should help in the process of generating new pictures, new conceptual understandings of the way we ought to interact with our surroundings. Only then can we proceed with laying the basis for building a productive community identity in the service of all in this country.

5. ADDRESSING THE BLIGHTED MUSLIM PSYCHE IN THE CONTEXT OF THE CURRENT WORLD CRISIS[1]

INTRODUCTION

We have been witnessing endless equivocation in response to the current world crisis that was brought on by the heinous attacks on the World Trade Centre in New York, followed by the unconscionable bombing of Afghanistan, whose people have endured decades of war.

What has not been forthcoming is a coherent and thoughtful response by South African Muslims to the impact of unfolding world events on the Muslim psyche. This chapter attempts to focus on the terms upon which Muslims should respond to their blighted psychological and moral dispositions.

It is based on two assumptions: the first is an admission that we are individually and collectively experiencing emptiness, conflicting emotions, stress, poor concentration and demotivation as a result of the confusion generated by world events, and the second is that our responses to these psychological deficits are inadequate, conflicting and even harmful to our ability to retain individual and communal cohesion and symmetry.

DEFENSIVENESS AND 'TURNING UP THE HEAT AND CANT'

A number of general responses have been forthcoming from Muslims. These have been marked by narrow defensiveness, which I contend is bereft of a vision and methodology to assist ordinary Muslims in this time of doubt and cynicism.

While the public discourse in the media, the office, shop floor and the school has been one of support and even sympathy, Muslims may have come to doubt the sincerity of their colleagues and even the views of their fellow faith adherents. In the crude world of stereotyped identity projections, where an either/or logic rules, one is allowed only two choices: either to support the Taliban or the West, with apparently no place for complexity and doubt.

Needless to say, in this climate Muslims have been experiencing difficulty in transacting normal and productive relations with others. We have generally been mediating the ramifications of the world crisis in silence without a network for support and comfort. We have not created a space to articulate our fears and concerns. We may have become less confident, more guarded and even confused about our role and purpose in our everyday business and civic lives.

Moreover, active participation in the broader unfolding of a productive South African citizenship has been placed on the backburner. Another type of response has been coming from small but vociferous groups scattered throughout the country. They

1 Published in the *Annual Review of Islam in South Africa*, 2001, Vol. 4, Centre for Contemporary Islam, UCT, based on a *khuṭbah* at CMRM, 26 October 2001.

have been projecting an outward defensiveness. Armed with a set of conspiracy theories, they have set out to defend what they perceive to be the slighted image of Islam. Asserting an oppositional logic, they have set about bashing the West and have come out in support of Bin Laden, the Taliban and their pre-modern, austere brand of Islamism. They have taken to the streets, with simple slogans and bravado. Some have even signed up for *jihād* in Afghanistan. Despite moments of 'radical' outpouring, they mostly carry on with their daily activities, oblivious of the contradiction in their continuing commitment to 'Western' consumer culture judging from their designer labels and gelled hair. Their opposition remains at the level of rhetoric, demonstrating a disjuncture between words and actions. In the face of confusion they have been turning up the 'heat and cant', where, instead of clarity, their reactions have caused confusion and disarray among ordinary Muslims.

The Qur'an refers to this type of behaviour as imbued with the 'fanaticism of ignorance' (*ḥamiyyah al-jāhiliyyah*), where reaction in the face of extreme social turbulence is informed by emotionalism and sentiment. In other words, this is a discourse that is devoid of intellectual and affective engagement. Such a position, while never popular, feeds a sense of demoralisation, and results in individuals and communities suffering lapses in confidence and moral conviction.

Another response has been forthcoming from the *ʿulamā* (Muslim religious leadership) and the pulpits. While a few have launched emotion-filled tirades, the responses of most of the imams have been muted and uncertain. Their hesitation could be attributed to a realisation that an emotional reaction on their part might lead to acts of indiscriminate violence by their younger congregants.

Many Imams, in responding to the perceived media onslaught on the image of Islam and its raison d'être, have been asserting Islam as a supreme worldview with answers to all the world's problems. While simplistic and unarticulated, this inverted triumphalism may be a natural psychological response, i.e. a re-assertion of one's basic commitments and convictions when the basis of one's faith seems to be undermined.

THE CONSEQUENCES OF DEFENSIVENESS

Defensiveness has, however, not provided Muslims with an adequate basis for counselling or pastoral care, based as it is on denial of our shortcomings and fault lines. It denies us the conceptual space to raise important and honest questions about the goings-on in the world and our complicity in them. Our suffering is never acknowledged and the pain of the community, the family and the individual is never spoken about or addressed directly.

The Qur'an refers to this type of community and individual suffering described above as the 'blaming soul' (*al-nafs al-lawwāmah*). My argument is that our individual and communal psychological dispositions are generally characterised by unacknowledged hurt and upheaval.

This disposition has been long in the making – at least 14 years – marked by the start of the first *intifādah* (uprising) in 1987, to the Gulf War in 1991 and the second Palestinian uprising in October 2000. During this period in South Africa we also witnessed brutal mass killings in the civil war between the United Democratic

Front and Inkatha, the Boipatong massacre in 1993, and Third Force train and other killings. The mass genocides in Rwanda and Bosnia have entangled us in a psychosis of violence and death. But it has been the brutal killing of hundreds of innocent Palestinians over the last year, coupled with the killing of innocents in Afghanistan, which have produced among Muslims intense feelings of helplessness and despair.

The spectre of Muslims dying has been visited upon us daily in our homes. We are watching images of violence and death on our television screens. We have become vicarious observers of human suffering. A feeling of helplessness is engendered by our inability to do anything concrete to alleviate this distant suffering. This dissociation between what we see and our inability to act, a kind of 'armchair suffering', induces feelings of social impotence akin to sexual impotence, which often seems to carry social as well as individual consequences. Social impotence threatens our sense of humanity – disabling us from acting productively, producing latent influences that work subliminally on our individual and collective psyches.

Our defensiveness is born out of a desire to retain a sense of dignity in the face of such helplessness. However, the denial about how we may be implicated in world events, or affected by their impact, prevents us from gaining a fresh perspective, making the necessary distinctions and identifying an adequate approach to this onslaught on our psyche. Denial produces a more perplexing and intractable situation.

MOVING BEYOND OUR DEFENSIVENESS

In a verse that captures at once the general ethos of the Qur'an, while directly addressing the 'blaming soul', Allah (SWT) declares: Say: O my servants who have transgressed against their souls! Despair not of the Mercy of God: for God forgives All sins: for He is Oft-Forgiving, Most Merciful (Q. 39:V53).

This verse points to the parameters of psychological and moral regeneration. It unequivocally declares that God's mercy and forgiveness are available to those who have degenerated or followed a destructive path. Allah extends a hand of forgiveness to those who approach Him with humility and recompense.

We should translate the 'hand' Allah extends to us into an honest examination of our weaknesses and fault lines. We should provide spaces for communal conversations and interaction, and offer each other support and comfort in a non-judgemental manner. While turning down the 'heat and cant' is an immediate necessity, building a culture of conversation and confidence requires long-term moral commitment. A counselling and pastoral approach involves a deeper struggle – *jihād al-nafs* (struggle over self) – conceptualised as a long-term project, which involves nurturing and support.

Cultivating respectful, non-judgemental conversations and relationships is crucial in building sophisticated and complex communities. Performing our *ʿibādāt* (acts of ritual worship) with renewed vigour and reflection is a starting point for connecting the inner self with the outer social self.

We have to cultivate the type of moral capacity (*taklīf*) that would enable us to distinguish between misguided responses to crises which fuel disorientation, and responses that attempt to creatively mediate the nuances of everyday life.

Finally, our task is to establish wholesome practices (*'amal al-ṣāliḥāt*) and institutions that will teach our children to function with creativity in a complex, multicultural world. Muslims are challenged to establish productive patterns of co-existence and interdependence, in the service of all, especially the poor, in South Africa.

The inspirational poem below by Muhammad Iqbāl (in Ṭufayl 1966), the Indian philosopher-poet, points the way to such a dynamic and courageous existence:

> I will reveal to you a point, bright as a pearl
>
> That you may distinguish between the slave and the free!
>
> The slave is by nature repetitive
>
> His experiences are bereft of originality!
>
> The free man is always busily creative,
>
> His bowstring is vibrant with new melodies!
>
> His nature abhors repetition;
>
> His pain is not like the circle traced by a compass!
>
> To the slave, time is a chain, His lips speak only of Fate!
>
> The courage of the free becomes a counsellor of Fate.
>
> His is the hand that shapes the events! (Iqbāl, 1938)

REFERENCE

Ṭufayl, M. 1966. *Iqbāl's Philosophy and Education.* Bazm-I-Iqbāl, University of California.

6. MUSLIM COMMUNITY SCHOOLS IN CAPE TOWN: EXEMPLIFYING ADAPTATION TO THE DEMOCRATIC LANDSCAPE[1]

INTRODUCTION

This chapter focuses on the establishment of schools by Muslim communities in Cape Town after 1994. The schools are registered with the Western Cape Education Department (WCED) as independent schools.[2] They are part of a nationwide trend that has seen a mushrooming of such schools all over the country, especially in the northern provinces.

This chapter is based on interviews with principals, teachers and governing body members of six high schools. It discusses the discursive rationales for establishing these schools and the ways in which particular governance modes have laid down the schools' operational parameters.[3]

These schools provide an apt focus for understanding the variegated ways in which Muslims in particular localities have been negotiating the unfolding post-apartheid democratic landscape. They are an expression of a confluence of global and local Islamisation discourses, mediated by changing discursive and material circumstances. The schools illustrate the complex ways in which religious discourses are given meaning and expression within local contexts.

MORAL PROPRIETY AS DISCURSIVE MARKER

The schools illustrate how members of one community have been engaging with the new democratic terrain. The need to provide a better quality education was given as a key reason by the majority of interviewees for setting up the schools. They referred to the deteriorating quality of education in public schools. They specifically emphasised the negative impact on poor schools by the ill-fated cutback of teachers, which had its most pernicious effect on coloured schools in Cape Town. Three of the principals and some of the teachers were senior educators at public schools. They took the handsome early retirement packages that were made available to entice

1 This chapter appeared in *Annual Review of Islam in South Africa*, Centre for Contemporary Islam, UCT, 2003, 6: 17-23.

2 The twelve schools established since 1994 are: Primary Schools: Al-Azhar (Township: Lotus River), Ambassador's College (Bridgetown), Sayyidina Bilal School (Khayelitsha), Hidayatul Islam (Kensington); High Schools: Belhar Education Centre (Belhar), Madrassatur Rajaa (Strand), Mitchells Plain Islamic High School (Rocklands); Schools from Grade One to Twelve: Darul Islam (Greenhaven), Ieglaasi Niyah (Beacon Valley), Islamia (primary school campus in Rylands and high school campus in Lansdowne), Maddrassatut Tarbiyah (Lotus River, girls and Parkwood, boys); SAMA (Sybrand Park, Grade 1, 2, 3 and 8, 9 and 10).

3 This chapter is part of a larger study I have done on these schools that focused on the hybrid mix of dynamics and discourses that constitutes meaning making and identity-construction processes in these schools.

teachers to leave the public sector. The majority of the teachers at these Muslim schools, though, are recently qualified teacher education graduates who were unable to find jobs in a shrunken teacher-employment market in public schools.

Perceptions about the collapse of quality education at public schools thus converged with teacher education market trends to give impetus for establishing the Muslim schools. The perceived breakdown of morality in townships and public schools provided the primary justification for establishing these schools. The interviewees voiced their concerns about the moral propriety of the students. Moral decay in townships was spoken about in negative terms as a sign of the overall moral relativism associated with secular democracy, as an apocalyptic sign of the nearing of *qiyāmah* (the Day of Reckoning). The government was variously referred to by one principal as "amoral" and as "aiding the work of the devil".

Public schools were described as breeding grounds for sin and vice, where children were socialised into sexual permissiveness, drug abuse and gang violence. It was particularly the governing body members' views about the adverse moral influence of the public schools that played a key role in producing negative perceptions about them. Being in direct competition with public schools, the Muslim community schools, in providing a moral alternative, also siphon off students from those public schools with which they are in direct competition.

During the interviews the negative perceptions of public schools and the weakening moral condition of society presented an opportunity to provide an education that would aim to nurture Islam-centred personalities. One principal reflected on the constitutional position "to place choices over morality in the hands of citizens. This is very threatening to people not used to this." Those interviewed indicated that in a country where morality had been strictly policed under apartheid, being given moral choice has had a disorienting impact. Muslim schools are expected to act as a bulwark against the creeping immorality of township life. The schools would be expected to provide their students with the attributes of an Islamic personality to withstand the onslaught against morality.

The schools were set up in an attempt to produce Islamic personalities in relative isolation from the perceived negative impact of their surrounding contexts. The schools can be regarded as a response to moral anxieties experienced by communities after 1994. The proponents of these schools have chosen 'splendid isolation' as a means of cultivating moral propriety among the students. The assumption is that these disengaged moral production processes would lay the foundation for children to interact with broader society.

SCHOOL GOVERNANCE AS A CHANNEL FOR BROADER COMMUNITY ADAPTATION PROCESSES

The mode of governance at each school indicates the ways broader community processes are relayed within these schools. Four governance types can be discerned, each constituted by a specific mode of community involvement.

Mosque-based governance

Three of the high schools can be described as mosque-based community schools. They are located within working-class to lower-middle-class coloured communities and are run by mosque-based community structures. A spirit of self-help, ideologically produced during mosque sermons, through the mobilising role of the shaykh or imām, and media resources such as pamphlets and community radio, serves to galvanise members around the need to retain communal cohesion and support. The schools' governing structures are made up of mosque-going, public-spirited community members who are active in fundraising and organisational activities. These schools were set up as part of a number of other social welfare activities, including burial services, financial assistance and afternoon religious classes for children who attend the public schools.

They help socialise the children into a communally-generated moral comportment and are crucial in reproducing the community's internal cohesion and adaptive vibrancy. The interviewees indicated a general reluctance to interact with other religious and civic groups in their environment. The internal cohesiveness of these communities seemed to be juxtaposed against the perceived negative influences of the external non-Muslim world. This lack of engagement also extended to their lack of enthusiasm for relating their organisational activities and discourses to broader civic and national citizenship processes. Few of the interviewees were attuned to the need to make linkages with the broader community and other faith and race groups.

These mosque-based schools play a central role in reproducing a discourse that distances their adherents from the surrounding community. Their school governance mode is thus based on a desire to establish a relatively isolated identity insulated from external influences and processes.

Governance as expatriate belonging

The second governance type is provided by the school that was set up by a number of Turkish expatriates who settled in Cape Town over the last decade. They are mostly professionals and business people. The principal of this school provided a dual rationale for establishing the school. He pointed out that the school was established because they wanted to provide their own children with a modern Muslim and Turkish-inspired education, on the one hand, while at the same time wanting to "share our educational resources with the people of this country", on the other. About seventy percent of the 134 children at the school are coloured Muslim, ten percent from the Cape Indian community, and twenty percent from the Turkish expatriate community. The school's governing body is made up of Turkish expatriates.

The school's operational discourse is framed around a constructive and progressive interaction with the secular democracy in South Africa. The school's symbolic environment, unlike that of the three mosque-based schools, indicates an eagerness to co-exist and interact with other communities. From my interviews, it seemed that this school is an example of an educational space where this expatriate community can socialise their children into a democratic South African environment.

This school's governance discourse could be said to represent an amalgam of three types of allegiance, i.e. sustaining a social network among Turkish expatriates in Cape Town, a demonstration of loyalty to their adopted country, and a display of religious solidarity with Muslims in Cape Town.

Governance as ideological closure

A school in an impoverished working-class area of the Cape Flats run by a group called the Tablīgh Jamāt provides the third governance type. Its governing body is made up of members of this group, teachers at the school, and a number of Tablīghī businessmen. Strict ideological control in line with the dictates of the group is achieved by the closed manner in which the school is governed.

The balance of control within the governing structure rests with the businessmen whose financial leverage gives them enormous sway in the running of the affairs of the Tablīgh group and the school. The businessmen, however, mostly reside in the northern province of Gauteng and in KwaZulu-Natal. This suggests that they have a 'remote control' type of governing influence. This influence is achieved relatively easily in the light of the group's strict ideological control, which provides very little scope for the principal and teachers to exercise autonomy in the running of the school.

This school is firmly framed by the generation of a distinct, narrow and disengaging ideological attitude among its students. They are socialised into adopting a narrow moral behavioural range that, according to the principal, is meant to insulate them from the corrupting influences of the modern world.

Governance as ethnicised identity production

A school that caters for middle-class to upper-middle-class children illustrates the fourth governance type. Its governing body is made up of mostly Indian professionals and business people. The children at the school come in more or less equal numbers from Indian and coloured Muslim families, who pay school fees of R8 000 per year. This compares with R6 500 paid at the 'Turkish expatriate' school, between R2 000 and R3 000 at the three mosque-based schools, and R1 200 at the Tablīghī school.

While all the schools in the study depend on community fundraising efforts such as big walks, food festivals and dinners to help fund expenses, the Indian-controlled school is able to depend on generous donations from its business community benefactors. Its expansive and modern campus, located in a middle-class suburb, is an example of the school's relatively easy access to financial support. The school is thus favourably positioned to compete in the student market with former white, now desegregated, public schools.

The school acts as a conduit for strong, though informal, business networks for members of the Indian business community. Business ties are sustained through the circulation of activities in and around the governance of the school. The interviewees spoke about the strategic ways in which people are included in and/or excluded from these networks. They aver that the networks are important in protecting access to certain markets and business opportunities.

The networks are restricted to certain carefully selected Indian business people and are relatively closed to their coloured Muslim counterparts, despite the large number of children from the coloured Muslim community at the school. This leads to intermittent, though muted, clashes between the governing body and the school's management and teachers involved in the internal processes in the school. The governing body was accused of standing in the way of having the school develop a flexible and mediated school environment. Teachers complained about not being supported to develop a curriculum and pedagogy that would enable the students to develop cross-cultural competence. Recognition of the cultural specificity of groups, instead of fluid cultural interaction, marks the governance discourse. One teacher suggested that this emphasis on "protecting the identity of the group may be motivated by the need to keep Indian and coloured students from fraternising too closely."

More generally, the governing body's subtle surveillance to discourage crossing group boundaries is informed by the need to protect its particular adaptive strategy in the new terrain. Reproducing a relatively closed Indian ethnic identity, kept in place by exclusive business networks, has placed particular limitations on the everyday operations at the school.

CONCLUSION

The governance modes of these schools are representative of broader adaptive strategies in the new democratic environment. The ways the different school governance types operate indicate how these schools are set up as a conduit of broader communal processes. Whether they are organised to serve narrow ideological purposes, community cohesiveness, expatriate belonging, or ethnic business interests (as described in each of the four types above), the schools' modes of governance play a key role in marking the discursive terrain within which these communal forms are being reproduced. The different governance types have structured the discursive terrain within schools in various ways. They have placed different constraints on local school processes, which have led to different in-school responses by principals and teachers.

The Muslim community schools are an example of the multiple ways in which religious communities adapt to the changing discursive environment, of the ways they read contexts strategically, and of how they adjust their symbolic and communal repertoires to invent new ways of existing in a changing context. Concerns about morality and quality have been appropriated to provide a rationale for the schools' establishment. The schools each represent different ways of adapting to their local environments. People as formative agents within local contexts interact with the discursive environment of the school to construct religious and social meanings. While the governance modes place certain parameters on the schools, the principals and teachers are actively involved in giving shape to the curriculum and pedagogical practices. The religious and educational meanings generated at these schools are thus the outcome of complex and fluid processes that are playing out within particular localities.

7. EDUCATIONAL REFLEXIVITY IN THE AGE OF DISCURSIVE CLOSURE[1]

The title I have given this presentation is *Educational reflexivity in the age of discursive closure*, which is intended to suggest that our educational activities, our intellectualism and our critical questions ought to be underpinned conceptually by the cultivation of educational and intellectual capacity and scholarship that would challenge the intellectual closure that characterises our religious discourses.

I suggest that our social practices as a community can only be fundamentally changed if we ask hard and careful questions about how religious power and practices are reproduced. The *farḍ kifāyah* – community responsibility – of a university such as IPSA is to provide a scholarly platform to cultivate new understandings and an intellectual base upon which new and invigorated social practices can emerge.

This presentation is therefore focused on the conceptual basis that I believe an institution such as an Islamic university should be founded on in generating educational reflexivity and conceptual capacity among its students. The students who train at this institution must be responsible, courageous and critical interlocutors in the social discourses and practices of the day.

When they leave IPSA, they must be able, in their various community roles, to guide their charges, their communities and their organisations in establishing appropriate and productive practices that can bring the Muslim community into greater alignment with broader local community processes in this city, this province and our country.

Towards the end of last year, when the establishment of this university was still being discussed, I sent an email to IPSA's principal, Shaykh Ighsaan Taliep, in which I expressed my scepticism about the idea to him. I suggested that the rationale for such a move must be based primarily on intellectualism and scholarship. I suggested to him that the foundations of a university should be the subject of vigorous debate.

My concern was based on my own experience as an academic at a higher education institution, the University of the Western Cape (UWC), where I did all my studies and am currently lecturing (until June 2009). South African higher education has been undergoing very fundamental transformative processes which I believe are threatening the system at its very core. Universities have been merged, they have to conform to equity profiles, their funding has been decreased, and they have to respond to a myriad of quality assurance and surveillance mechanisms.

UWC is experiencing somewhat of an identity crisis. The government's funding formula suggests all universities should be equally proficient in research and scholarship, on the one hand, and teaching and learning, on the other. On this view, UWC should become a world-class university and while we take this ambition

1 This chapter is based on a paper presented in 2005 at the International Peace College South Africa (IPSA) and published in the 2005 edition of the IPSA journal.

seriously, we do realise that we may never achieve it. Instead, I fear that we may end up becoming a poor carbon copy of a fully research-led university.

To resolve this impasse I suggested that UWC should actively set out to become a top-class undergraduate teaching university with excellent teaching and academic support and development programmes for working-class students in the Western Cape. Providing access to poor students for academic training in technology, economics, law, science, the humanities and education would form the basis of our academic project.

In addition, we should then build research expertise at Masters and doctoral level in recognised niche areas in which we have top-flight academic infrastructure and expertise. These niche areas can only operate if the academics in them have sustainable research programmes and are publishing in national and international journals. UWC has a number of these niche academics. But we should ask hard questions about the balance between teaching and research, cut where appropriate and strengthen where needed. There are at the moment important intellectual debates going on all over the campus to determine the direction we might follow in the coming years.

How would these kinds of debates play themselves out at a newly functioning, privately funded university in the Cape such as IPSA? I was concerned that if this university was to go down, if it must close, we would not only have wasted valued resources and intellectual energy, but it would have a very demoralising effect on our community psyche. Our confidence about our place in Cape Town and the world may suffer, and our intellectual boldness may diminish as a result.

What started out as scepticism has for me suddenly become a question of necessity. How do people like me who are based at public universities engage with IPSA in a responsible and critical manner in order to play a role in strengthening and directing it along a productive academic path? How do we become inclusive of attempts to build IPSA as an intellectual project, instead of sniping dismissively, like armchair Trotskyites, from the sidelines?

It has been indicated to me that IPSA's series of seminars will ask important questions about Islam and Muslim practices in our growing democracy. This is an important intellectual initiative, acting as a catalyst for this university to substantiate its scholarly agenda.

Where are our young community intellectuals in the Muslim community currently being produced? By community intellectuals I mean those young people who establish their activism and their moral capacity in thoughtful, critical and new ways of community struggle. Are we reproducing these types of young people, or are our institutions producing people more interested in the necessary, but not sufficient, ceremonial or salvation side of their community engagement?

The Cape Muslim community has produced two types of community activists, both the outcome of our intellectual modernisation during the twentieth century: one is what I'll call the intellectual community Imam and the other the Muslim activist intellectual. Shaykh Ismail Ganief (died 1958) is an example of the intellectual community Imam. As Hoosain Ebrahim's (2004) fascinating book on the life of the Shaykh illustrates, he was very well versed in the traditional disciplines of Islam.

He became an inspiring teacher, author and community leader of note. He was also an inheritor of a long line of religious leaders, *'ulamā'*, in Cape Town.

He produced many other imams, including Imam Abdullah Haron and Imam Ismail Johnstone (1935-1993). Imam Haron was an ordinary Imam-about-town, a snappy dresser and a rugby and cricket supporter. He was propelled into political struggle because of his moral sensitivity in response to the injustices of apartheid, and in no small part also by his interaction with the young Muslim college and university graduates of Claremont during the 1950s and 1960s. Imam Haron has without any question and deservedly become the face of the Muslim resistance against the oppression of apartheid.

Imam Johnstone, about whom a book surely must be written, inspired many people with his leadership, educational activities and his Arabic teaching. He taught many young people who went on to attend both secular and Islamic universities. Many of them have become leading community figures all over Cape Town.

The Muslim activist intellectual tradition emerged in the 1940s and 1950s. A number of first-generation Muslim young people graduated from higher education institutions during these decades. As my project on Muslim teachers shows, most of them were politicised by the stringent anti-collaborationist tradition of the Non-European Unity Movement. They were thus heavily politicised, but unlike my grand-uncle Ali Fataar (see Wieder and Fataar 2003), and his contemporary comrades Cissie Gool and Goolam Gool, this newer generation of Muslim intellectuals of the 1950s attempted a synthesis between their radical anti-state politics and their Islamic commitments. These young people were reading important modern Islamic literature such as the works of Ḥassan al-Banna (1906-1949), Mawdūdī and Quṭb.

They began to develop a critique of the Muslim community, its dominant discourses, its intellectual complacency, but most of all its political quiescence. They were impatient with the compliant attitude of the *'ulamā'* to the politics of apartheid that were unfolding in the 1950s. They established the District Six Muslim Youth Movement and the Claremont Muslim Youth Association with the express purpose of politicising the community.

They were targeted by some *'ulamā* from the *mimbar* (pulpit) for 'mixing Islam with politics'. They were man-handled [sic] and thrown out of mosques, vilified and called donkeys. They struggled to establish a foothold in the community. Abu Bakr Fakir (1938-2002), a young Claremont resident in the 1950s and a secularly trained person who was mostly self-taught in *Fiqh* and Arabic, was an example of these young people's attempts to operate on the terrain of the *'ulamā*. He wrote, printed and published the acclaimed *Manual of Prayer and Fasting* (Fakir 1978) in the mid-1970s.

One of the most important contributions these young people made was to establish a new discourse, ask new questions, and postulate new ways of imagining their community. Their legacy only became concretised in the mid-1980s, when a younger generation of Muslim activists in the Call of Islam, the Muslim Students Association, Muslim Youth Movement and Qibla emerged out of the cauldron of the student and youth uprisings of the time. They too asked challenging new questions of this community, built organisational infrastructure, entered into alliances with other community organisations, and generally dragged the community, kicking and screaming, into the broader anti-apartheid Cape Town body politic.

The current Premier, Ebrahim Rasool, who was a Muslim activist in the Call of Islam and the United Democratic Front, was part of a group of young people who contributed enormously towards shifting the community's discourse. This was based on a number of strategic considerations that guided the political mobilisation of Muslims to join the mass democratic struggles of the 1980s and 1990s. The 1980s activists learnt from the mistakes of the radicals of the 1950s. They did not alienate the *ʿulamā*, instead choosing to build the *ʿulamā's* confidence in their own leadership role, while bringing them into the anti-apartheid movement.

In highlighting the various developments around Muslim community activism, I want to suggest that the young people's intellectual courage was part of a different social context, which emerged under apartheid, the reaction to it, the community's modernisation, the radical politics of the 1950s and beyond. This was a different world. Islamic universities in South Africa were not on the horizon. Our adaptive reflexivity in the 1980s and 1990s emerged out of this milieu, shaping our discourses, informing our community responses, and ultimately conditioning our complex and ambiguous stances within the broader anti-apartheid context.

The question that confronts us today revolves around what our reflexivity should be based on. The prior questions are: How should we understand the challenges that confront us today? What role should a university or any of our other educational institutions play in building this reflexivity?

It is in this light that IPSA's choice to become a university is instructive and courageous, signalling clearly that its establishment is an attempt to provide a platform to interrogate these types of issues[2]. Why do I say so? IPSA could very easily have chosen to be a *Dār al-ʿulūm* (a theological seminary), where the production of *ʿulamā* would have been primary. I would suggest that while IPSA will be producing *ʿulamā,* the notion of a university is clearly suggestive of the desire to establish a broad and open-ended intellectual platform for its intellectual position.

The following question therefore has to be asked: How and on what conceptual basis can a four-year Bachelor of Theology degree be accomplished based on this open-ended intellectual platform? And while I believe this question will primarily be asked in curriculum development committees of the university, i.e. what content should be covered, whether the four Sunni *Fiqh* schools will be taught, or whether the other minority schools of thought will be introduced in the 3rd and 4th year, whether *Fiqh* will be taught in Arabic to facilitate Arabic language acquisition, which may result in a lower level of intellectual substance?

Other curriculum and pedagogical questions will revolve around whether a doctrinaire approach to *madhāhib* (schools of Islamic jurisprudence) will be followed, whether the students will be encouraged to do their own research, and whether they will be expected to present formulaic and rote answers, or whether students will

2 IPSA subsequently registered as a college on the South African Higher Education Qualifications Framework, although the idea of becoming a university is still being pursued.

be rewarded for independent thinking and the ability to develop their own voices and opinions.

IPSA will also be confronted with the challenges posed by the academic capacity of the first-year students, whether the academic development (AD) and intellectual preparation of the students should be a part of the curriculum, whether AD should be offered just to under-prepared students, or whether, because of the widespread lack of academic preparation, AD should be mainstreamed.

Given all these important curriculum questions that the university would face day to day in the lecture theatres and in the curriculum meetings, the key conceptual issue for me is how IPSA will respond over the next few years to the question: What type of intellectual or scholarly identity should a university such as IPSA assume in this critical period in the life of Cape Town and South Africa?

In my attempt to provide a conceptual map in response to this question, I would like to suggest the university should aim to cultivate, in a creative and an intellectually substantiated and patient manner, a discourse that will help us break through our normal everyday existence, one that will allow us to view the world in a different and more enabling light, that will move this community from intellectual and social complacency to an intense grappling with the complex world that we are living in, and to develop the capacity to encounter that world with fortitude, intellectual openness and creativity.

REFERENCES

Ebrahim, M.H. 2004. *Shaykh Ismail Hanif Edwards: His Life and Works,* Paarl, Paarl Print.

Fakir, A. 1978. *Manual of Prayer and Fasting,* Wynberg, Rustica Press.

Wieder, A. & Fataar, A. 2003. "Education, Radical Politics and Modernity in southern Africa: The Teaching Life of Ali Fataar" in *Southern African Review of Education,* 8(1):31-45.

8. DEVELOPING A CRITICAL MUSLIM POLITICAL ENGAGEMENT WITH SOUTH AFRICAN REALITIES[1]

I approach this topic with some trepidation and a heightened sense of responsibility. I suspect I was asked to talk today because I publicly commented on radio in the negative about whether it is wise for *'ulamā* (religious leaders) groups to support political parties. I will come to that directly later in the presentation.

The main argument I will make today is based on my view that Muslims in this country must now act 'counter-intuitively' against our historically defined Cape Sunnah, our public discourses, to establish our relevance to the complex challenges of the post-apartheid period. Acting counter-intuitively means we should act contrary to what common sense suggests. But it has another meaning: 'to act on impulse against better judgement'. I want to suggest that our 'better judgement' or our 'common sense' should now perhaps be challenged fundamentally.

My approach to this presentation is based on the qur'anic notion of *shūrā,* which is interpreted as inter-subjective and inclusive dialogue. Such dialogue, I believe, is defined by an intellectual disposition, an *adab* (ethics) based on inclusion and respect for heterodox and diverse opinions. *Shūrā,* or inter-subjective dialogue and engagement, is also my conceptual framework for today's presentation, a way of thinking about, and engaging in the politics of the day.

I will suggest that Muslim life and its political expressions are formulated in the context of a swirl of discourses, both from inside and outside the Muslim community. I will also argue against viewing the political positions we take in oppositional and exclusive terms. Our discourse must not be adversarial, as simply the outcome of us-them contests, set up in victim or perpetrator terms with the labels of 'modernist', 'radical' or 'sell-out' merely intended to shut down debate. This leaves no space for productive engagement.

I am interested in a reading of Cape Muslim history that engages with its continuities and discontinuities, its internally defining struggles, its cross-cutting influences, and the diverse currents that make up Muslim public discourse.

LIVING IN COMPLEX TIMES

Let me start by saying that we now live in complex times. The dual features of globalisation and constitutional democracy now work together to construct the outlines of our lives. It affects what we become as a community, how we see ourselves, how we communicate, how we do business, whom we marry, where our kids work, whether in South Africa, Europe, Australasia or the Middle East.

---

1 This chapter is based on a presentation delivered at the International Peace College South Africa in March 2009. It was published as a chapter in Fataar, A. and Esack, F. eds. 2009, *After the Honeymoon: Muslim Religious Leadership and Political Engagement in a Post-Apartheid South Africa*. Cape Town, Centre for Progressive Islam.

We have been joined by fellow Muslims and others from the African continent and beyond, who have come to enrich our religious tapestry, even if they have not quite assimilated into the mainstream of the community. Many families have settled in Cape Town from South Africa's northern provinces. Many diverse and heterodox Islamic influences have entered the city and solidified their presence. For example, the Naqshabandi Tarīqah (Sufī order) has found fertile soil in Cape Town, the Tijāniyyah Tarīqah has established a presence, people aligned to the Murābiṭūn bought a famous church in a prominent location in downtown Cape Town and turned it into a mosque, and the Ahl al-Bayt Shi`a community now has an organised presence in Cape Town. The increasing number of African Muslims challenges us to become less race-obsessed and more inclusive. And the influx of refugees and migrants from African countries and beyond have turned Cape Town into a social and cultural melting pot.

One way of understanding the Muslim community of Cape Town is through its multiple accommodations within the broader South African contexts over the centuries. As a community we have always endeavoured, as other communities do, to establish the best situation for our survival and acculturation in Cape Town. These accommodations, of finding a level of relative social and political comfort, were disrupted from time to time.

The community, however, managed to remain fairly cohesive, if marginal to the travails of the other oppressed groups in the city. But perhaps this picture is too simple. It hides from view the fissures and fractures that form part of our community's co-existence with the rest of the city. It hides the fact that the community has found an accommodation that has enabled us in general to adopt a politically quiescent attitude towards the apartheid state. I think here of the example of the collusion between I.D. du Plessis, the apartheid ideologue, in charge of Coloured Affairs and some Cape Muslims who attempted to construct an ethnic Malay identity from the 1940s through the 1950s. It did not come as a surprise that the pall bearers at Du Plessis's funeral were suitably attired 'Malay' men who carried his coffin into church.

That was the Cape Town that was, and is still; made up of a diverse Muslim polity; culturally hybrid, exciting, politically accommodating, and in some instances quietly complicit, while at other times politically courageous.

ACTING COUNTER-INTUITIVELY

Let me be clear. The presentation of Cape Town's Muslims as active opponents of the apartheid state is a post-apartheid construction, a myth. The young people in the Claremont Muslim Youth Association and the District Six Muslim Youth Movement during the 1950s would have disagreed with such a construction, and so would the youth of the 1970s and the 1980s in the Qibla Mass Movement, the Call of Islam, the Muslim Student Association and the Muslim Youth Movement.

The main point I want to make today is that we should as a community proceed counter-intuitively. We should challenge our historical ties to seeking accommodation with those who hold power in our city, province and country. In other words, we should also be open to critically questioning the accommodations that we have been making as a community in the past and into the post-apartheid period.

Our mainstream political responses have not sought to pose problems or trouble our historically framed accommodations with reference to those in power. We have sought instead to accommodate ourselves to the new political situation, related to it somewhat as a minority and not as a key constituent part of this city. I, therefore, want to suggest that the way we have responded is probably consistent with our historical search for accommodation to context, geography and power, instead of challenging power and thereby helping to define the political temper in the city and the country.

Acting counter-intuitively against aspects of our Cape Town *Sunnah* (tradition), means that we now have to figure out what matters most to ordinary people struggling to make ends meet as they endure daily hardships in their attempts to establish dignified livelihoods.

This struggle is located in the realm of *ijtihād*, which is intellectual exertion, based on research scholarship into the ways we live in the city. This could be pursued by students and researchers at IPSA, and programmes in Islamic studies at Cape Town's universities. The search for new modes of existence should also be based on *jihād*, which in this case refers to moral struggle or praxis that connects us to the material, political and symbolic challenges of the time. We have to think and act outside of our predefined boxes. But we have to interrogate and challenge how these boxes have acquired their shape and intellectual substance.

We have perhaps become comfortable with our consorting with power. We have never been the leading partner in this dance with power. We are not even sometimes sure whether we are actually dancing or maybe jogging, or running backwards. Our accommodations or political responses may have been driven by elite class interests, the interests of those people who are visible, who make themselves visible, and perhaps not by the real interests of the poor and marginal in the city. Elite interests, whether driven by prominent families, business, well-positioned mosques, prominent *murīd* (congregants) and religious institutions, have determined this accommodation to find a narrow comfort zone, relatively insulated from broader struggles.

The tight connection between some religious actors, business and politics over the last few years exemplifies how this accommodation works. One could mention a few interesting examples of this connection in the Muslim community. The post-apartheid period has ushered in space for greater mobility and material acquisition. The increase in material wealth in the middle-class sectors of the community has been quite spectacular. One simply has to stand on Kromboom Road running through the Athlone-Rondebosch East belt to observe the 'wealth on wheels' on display, those Muslims in their expensive brand new SUVS and luxury vehicles who pass by.

The middle classes and the religious elites are probably most invested in political accommodation and therefore will lobby hard for the conditions necessary to access contracts, prominent jobs and black economic empowerment deals. Politicians are implicated in this and some religious actors chase the same ideals. Islamic financing, for example, has never been in a more vibrant space. Most financial institutions, with their Islamic advisors in tow, and their latest halal-friendly investment products on offer, are competing for a piece of the large Muslim financial pie.

It stands to reason that these elites do not want a political climate that paints Muslims in a bad light as opponents of democracy and the ruling government. It would simply be bad for business. However, the increase in the material poverty of at least 30% of the Muslim community in this city has been staggering. Many Muslims live in increasing hardship, struggling to make ends meet. I observed this in my ethnographic research in a prominent township, where I witnessed Muslims, like other township dwellers, having to adapt to conditions of unemployment, the hold of the criminal economy, and a surge in single-parent homes.

What does the *Fiqh al-Aqaliyyāt* (a legal discourse alert to minority contexts) mean in this context? A *fiqh* of minorities currently focuses too narrowly on questions of identity, based as it is on the experiences of the Muslims who migrated to the first world, in London, Amsterdam, Paris and Barcelona. The key difference between minorities in Europe and South Africa is that we do not have an identity problem in South Africa, at least not yet. Muslims in Europe are regarded as third-class citizens. They are neither accepted as properly European, nor are they accepted in their countries of origin as properly Middle Eastern Muslim. They struggle with an in-between identity. Muslims in South Africa are as old as the first colonial settlements in this country. I disavow a minority identity which requires preferential treatment with special narrow concerns and fears. I prefer a *fiqh* that is responsive to the plight of the marginalised and the poor, concerned with political critique and challenge, a *fiqh* committed to the everyday battles to survive and adapt in contexts of material brutalisation.

SECURING A NEW POLITICS

But how do we secure a new politics? The accommodation that we have sought in the post-apartheid era is not benign. The alignment between politics, business and religious elites is governed by self-interest as much as by the concern for the public good. I am not so naïve as to suggest that we should rail against this alignment or oppose it with all our might. That would be a sort of 'political fundamentalism of a special type', the type that says we should not get involved in business or politics, or deny the linkages that exist between politics, religion and business. These linkages are the life-blood of any community. What I am suggesting is that Islam demands that we privilege a confrontation with the bigger ethical challenges of the moment. Self-interest has to be trumped by broader commitments: by an incorruptible politics tied to the interests of the most marginal in society.

But the question remains: How do we develop different political responses as a community informed by concerns with the needs of the marginalised. These include persons living with HIV and AIDS inside and outside the Muslim community, those who sleep in shacks, those who fast involuntarily every day, not just during the month of Ramaḍān, those children who now grow up in single families or with parents who are under- or unemployed, who attend deprived schools, young people who grow up on their own, without the cultural codes and regulative order that older people normally provide.

How then do we as a community 'speak truth to power' in the face of these dramatic challenges? How do we develop inter-subjective dialogue, spaces for critique that questions our internal responses and challenges those in power? How do we criticise and built alternative pictures and possibilities of a better life for all? I assume that these are the questions that we now have to confront courageously, critically and inclusively. The challenge of leadership is to create the conditions for such an active dialogue.

But let us get to the heart of the matter. What is the problem that we are addressing here today?

Fourteen years into the democratic period our country begs for answers to some very fundamental questions: Have we lost our political compass? Are we violating our country's Constitution? Are we reneging on the expectation to deliver a socially just country for all who live in it? Following from these questions, have our communities and religious structures been playing a critical and constructive role in the quest for a better life for all? And are our religious and civic formations playing a watchdog role in keeping government accountable?

The question about whether *ʿulamā* groups should support political parties is for me a reflection of the heightened sensitivity about both government failure and our own neglect to keep those in power accountable.

Let me list some government and party political failures:

- The current mobilisation against the National Prosecution Authority and the Scorpions;
- The raping of the justice system by elements in the ruling party;
- The rising rates of tuberculosis in the Western Cape;
- The corrupt ties to the arms deal and corruption generally;
- Failure in the areas of housing, health, safety, security and education.

Have we spoken against these failures? Have we challenged those in power and kept them accountable? Have we held ourselves accountable by way of a proper developmental response to these challenges? I would like to suggest that being too close to power has prevented us from speaking 'truth to power' and from doing what matters to alleviate the plight of our people. The question is whether we are fulfilling our Allah-ordained role, whether we even recognise our prophetic responsibility. Finding very few answers inside the house of Islam for these questions, let me reach to the outside for some indication of what this prophetic role might be.

Dr Allan Boesak recently provided a critique of the government. His language was reminiscent of a United Democratic Front (UDF) mass rally in the 1980s. Many people related to the speech with nostalgia, remembering the vision of hope we had for the new South Africa, and how this vision has been betrayed. But Boesak did not go far enough. He spoke in very general terms about the abuse of power by the ruling elite, calling for a return to mass mobilisation. Boesak's critique never went beyond generalities.

Let me turn to the critique of the abuse of political power by Prof. Sam Maluleke, the President of the South African Council of Churches when he recently delivered the annual Desmond Tutu lecture at the University of the Western Cape. Maluleke probed into the heart of power. He criticised the church for shirking its responsibility by failing to speak truth to power. He was particularly harsh about the role of the church in post-apartheid South Africa. He pointed out that "church leaders spend their time waiting for that call – not the call from heaven, but the call from the Union Buildings or Luthuli House". He suggested that the church "was in danger of becoming not merely a training ground, but a playground of politicians ... the church was now available for politicians to use and abuse, to command and to call. This is the reason the church is often silent, when it should be speaking, absent where it should be present, tongue-tied when the nation is hungry for words".

Does this also apply to us in the Muslim community? Are we also absent where we should be present, tongue-tied when the nation is hungry for our words? If Maluleke suggests that the church has become the state at prayer, maybe we have become the state at *du'a* (supplication)? Where are our critical voices? Are we too close to power? Have those in power out-manoeuvred us, provided us jobs, contracts and BEE deals? Have we chosen to remain silent for fear of jeopardising our access to these goodies? Have we externalised our voices towards faraway places where Muslim are oppressed? There can be no doubt that Muslims in Palestine, Iraq, Iran and Afghanistan need our support. But have we used the plight of these people far away as a proxy, a stand-in, for ignoring the oppression nearby, on our doorsteps?

CONCLUSION – SPEAKING TRUTH IN CLEAR TERMS TO POWER

In conclusion, let me return to the main theme of this presentation. Muslims have to seriously challenge their comfortable accommodation to power. This is now a *farḍ kifāyah* (communal obligation), an urgent community responsibility.

IPSA's role in organising these critical seminars is one necessary step. Its research agenda could be based on understanding how Muslims now live in the post-apartheid period. Such research would be valuable for understanding how religious institutions, teachers and Imams could go about addressing the needs of their students and congregants.

I have suggested that our Cape *Sunnah,* our public discourses, run deep. It will require deep intellectual and practical engagement for us to act differently. We should not deny the burden of history, but we should not simply live in its image.

Needless to say, I find support for political parties 'sanctified' by religious groupings unacceptable. People ought to make their political choices politically, not influenced by *'ulamā* groupings. We should counsel to all our people across the widest range of political opinions.

But we cannot be neutral about the broader ethical issues. To act counter-intuitively now requires us to develop the ability to speak truth to power, in blunt and clear ways when the situation demands it, and at other times in nuanced and constructive ways. As I have suggested, this should be done inter-subjectively, in rigorous, on-going and inclusive dialogue. This requires that we protect each other's right to hold heterodox views, without name-calling or labelling.

My bias is towards a dialogue governed by an imagination that imagines our city, our country and the world differently, based on the qur'anic principles of truth (*ḥaqq)* and justice *('adl).*

9. EDUCATIONAL ADAPTATION IN A CHANGING CITY[1]

In the brutal apartheid years, our educational initiatives galvanised a public-spiritedness that saw the emergence of viable Islamic communities and educational institutions all over the Cape Flats.

The post-apartheid city has unleashed enormous destabilising and creative energies as people search for appropriate schools, *madrasas* and educational experiences for their children. It is now a fact that most of the city's children, across the class spectrum, are severely affected by what is perceived to be a faltering public school system.

Apartheid education has bequeathed us an enormously uneven legacy and the post-apartheid dispensation has failed to produce a unified education system of quality. This has had enormous consequences for where our children go to school, the educational experiences they have while attending their schools of choice, and the implications for family and community functioning.

Children with educational aspirations move across the city to access their schools of choice. This leads to the severance of the crucial link between school-going and community living, making children less rooted and less committed to their community, neighbourhoods and religious or traditional commitments. This phenomenon expresses itself, for example, in the Muslim community by way of the burgeoning Muslim private and community school sector in the city, the growth of Qur'an memorisation (*ḥifẓ*) schools and home schooling options.

People are in search of an elusive good education, which they imagine will serve as a moral bulwark against the encroaching secular order and its implied moral corruption. While growth in the diversity of schools has been one outcome, we seem to struggle to tie schooling to the common socialisation of all of our country's children into a cohesive public culture. Educational arrangements are now institutional purveyors of group identity, ethnocentricity, religious parochialism and even racism.

Our *madrasa* system has also been re-arranged. It is now largely accepted that *madrasa* education no longer plays the strong socialising role that it once did, having to compete with the time-consuming activities that our children are involved in at their schools, as well as with children's immersion in information technologies, social media and peer associations that stretch across the city, beyond the immediate neighbourhood.

In other words, the coordinates of our children's educational processes have been rearranged, often in the absence of an awareness of the precariousness involved in these processes. There is now increased anxiety about our children's educational future. We have noticed the creeping unemployment prospects of uneducated young people, and we have calculated that getting our children into the right schools is

1 Published in *Al-Mizan*, Newsletter of the Claremont Main Road Mosque, *ʿĪd al-Fitr* edition, August 2012 / 1433. 2(1): p. 12.

now one of our most important preoccupations. We invest large sums of money in school fees, extramural activities and tutorial support. We travel long distances to get our children to school, sports practice, matches and cultural events in the hope of providing them with a positional advantage, entry to the right university, and middle-class jobs.

Most of this is done on credit, loan and onerous debt arrangements with educational institutions. We have to contend with newer and harsher levels of survival and adaptation as the impact of multiple economic crises kick in and unemployment rises. We now live our lives in a context of rising domestic poverty and unstable domestic arrangements.

Life is now experienced on the basis of generalised anxiety, greater worry and stress, amid increased levels of material deprivation. Our children exercise their educational aspirations in a harsh material world with great expectations and precariousness, in the hope of accessing a successful life.

And we struggle as a community to engage in civic-minded conversations about common productive living. Absent from our educational discourses are deliberations about socially just lifestyles, anti-racist and anti-sexist practices, and environmental justice. There are very few spaces for meaningful deliberation about Islamically prescribed values of neighbourliness and respect for diversity. And, because of increasing individualism and the striving to enter middle-class lifestyles, we have not been responding productively as a Muslim community to the poverty that besets our city.

Where do we cultivate the necessary values and dispositions for a pro-poor sensibility, anti-racist and anti-sexist living, and a commitment to sustainable futures, if not in our schools, our mosques and *madrasas*? It seems then that we are now challenged to redirect our intellectual energies away from an ethnocentric focus on our individual preoccupations, or a narrow focus on our selves or exclusive group preservation.

We do not have to succumb to the often elusive scramble for a middle-class lifestyle, at the expense of greater concern for the wellbeing of all. We now have to develop an intellectual and educational platform that will mitigate some of the negative features of our atomistic, ego-driven lifestyles.

More importantly, we have to ignite a conversation about ethical living in this city, and what better place to start than in respect of our educational endeavours. We have to force a more responsive conversation about the nature of our ethical responses, in our mosques, public media and educational institutions.

At the family and personal level, we have to establish productive family routines and conversations about productive living. At the *madrasa* level, it would mean augmenting and supplementing our rote-learning pedagogies with critical, interactive ones. Children have to cultivate the ability to interpret and adapt to the challenges of contemporary times.

This is not a time for anti-intellectualism or a retreat into intellectual laziness. Countering individualism and ego-driven behaviour can only be done by cultivating a responsive intellectual orientation that addresses the complexity of our times.

10. MUSLIM ELITES, THE 'ULAMĀ AND AMBIGUOUS ACCOMMODATION IN DEMOCRATIC SOUTH AFRICA[1]

In March 2009 I wrote a paper based on a presentation at IPSA in which I called for a politics of critique and critical dialogue among Muslims in South Africa (see Chapter 8 in this book). I responded to what I described as the easy accommodation to the prevailing political situation that was established by dominant Muslim groupings in democratic South Africa. I decried the lack of critical internal dialogue.

The paper elicited some interesting responses. Prof. Farid Esack and I eventually produced a book which included responses to my paper by a range of social actors in the Muslim community.

The call for a debate on a critical attitude to current-day politics fell on fertile ground. There was much to question about the direction of our democratic politics, and the uneven and difficult terrains of social justice, specifically how our government's politics seemed to compromise on social justice commitments.

My 2009 paper seemed to find resonance in calling for a politics of challenge instead of acquiescence and simple acceptance among Muslims. A politics of acquiescence often manifested in the service of newly aligned class interests in the Muslim community.

What left me exasperated is what I have now come to understand as my lack of proper characterisation of the nature and specific outlines of the politically accommodating attitude among Muslims. From the perspective of my then somewhat trenchant but fairly simplistic call for 'speaking truth to power' the world looked very simple.

There are deeper questions to consider: Why have Muslim publics, by and large, come to adopt such an accommodating attitude to our politics? How does one understand the make-up of our civic politics?

How and on what conceptual basis do we understand and engage in productive processes aimed at a politics of critical challenge informed by social justice?

These are my framing concerns, although I won't address them directly. Instead, I'll take you through a set of conceptual stances that may enable us to understand aspects of Muslim democratic imaginaries in South Africa.

---

1 This chapter is based on a presentation that I gave at the University of Johannesburg, in July 2014. It draws on an article that I co-authored with Prof. Sindre Bangstad, entitled 'Cape Muslims and Post-Apartheid Politics', published in the *Journal of Southern African Studies*, Vol. 36, No.4, 2010. I also drew liberally, and with permission from the author, on an unpublished article by Imām al-Ustādh Prof. Ebrahim Moosa entitled 'Genealogy of Muslim Religious Discourse and Constitutional Democracy: The Case of South Africa's Muslim Minority' (unpublished, 2010).

Let me start out with a simple set of juxtapositions:

1. In 1882 Abdol Burns (born c.1838), a Muslim leader, told the Cape Town city council that if he was forced to choose between the prescriptions of his religion and the secular municipal laws of the coloniser, he would submit to the claims of his religion. "My religion," Burns proclaimed, "is superior to the law."
2. In 1969 Imam Haron was killed in detention by the South African police. An *ʿulamā* group declared, "If Imam Haron died because of Islam, we stand fully by him." Here the signifier 'if' signals this group's probable lack of support for Imam Haron if he had been killed because of politics.
3. On 25 June 2008 Mawlānā Ighsaan Hendricks (1964-2018), the President of the largest and most influential *ʿulamā* organisation in South Africa, the Muslim Judicial Council (MJC), asserted after a meeting with the African National Congress's President, Jacob Zuma, that "MJC members would welcome Zuma as president of our country".

These three statements are varied expressions of one theme, i.e. the relationship between religious conscience and secular political arrangements. The first two portend some kind of separation between religion and politics, while the third seems to collapse religious conscientiousness into political support. Here we see conscience juxtaposed or intertwined with personal law or secular constitutionalism.

Notre Dame University Professor of Islam, Ebrahim Moosa, suggests that while conscience does have a place within a constitutional order, there are always concerns that the arbitrary exercise of conscientiousness could undermine the rule of law. The rule of law, in turn, requires strong enforcement measures. In the context of the outbreak of a smallpox epidemic, the colonial authorities wanted to pursue a policy of universal vaccination, which Burns rejected from a purported religious perspective. He concocted the view that 'vaccination was against the sharia '.

While we can only speculate as to Burns's motives, Moosa's analysis inspires one to ask several questions, such as: Was Burns's statement emblematic of the incommensurability of competing norms where secular norms are pitted against religious norms? Would he have opposed the municipal law with a similar vehemence if it were derived from the sharia? Is it wise for government to force citizens to make a choice between their religious values and their civic commitments?

Burns raised the central question in matters of constitutionalism: What are the limits of the authority and powers of the government?

What I want to point out is that Burns's position was not a mere rejection of constitutionalism or the secular colonial dispensation. It can be read more as a specific articulation and deployment of the dance between religious conscience and secular law.

After all, very soon after he led a mini-rebellion – the so-called cemetery uprisings in the 1880s – for which he was jailed, he attempted to run, unsuccessfully, for municipal elections on the basis of his newly acquired acclaim.

Similarly, the mainstream's reaction to Imam Haron's death was an expression of the depth of political apathy and fear that prevailed among Cape Muslims and their leadership as much as it was a rejection of Haron's politics or the need to guard against the conflation of religion and politics.

The current MJC president's support for Zuma represents a drift across the religion-politics line, i.e. the discursive line between religion and politics that was drawn in the sand during the apartheid years.

This line always seemed to exist. During apartheid, the dividing line was maintained as a means of justifying some kind of accommodation of the apartheid state.

This did not mean that this line was not crossed in all sorts of ways. An example of such a crossing was the collaboration by some Cape Town shaykhs with apartheid Coloured Affairs arrangements.

In 2008, though, Mawlānā Hendricks crossed the line emphatically. In so doing, the leader of a religious body which had more or less consistently defined itself as apolitical and concerned largely with religious matters throughout the apartheid period seemed to indicate that the MJC would tie its flag to the ANC mast – even if its own members and Muslim constituencies in the Western Cape remained sharply divided over such a stance.

Hendricks's stance, however, was not met with the same vehemence as the outcry that met then MJC president Shaykh Nazeem Mohamed's (d. 2000) momentary flirtation with the United Democratic Front in the 1980s.

What is therefore clear is that certain Muslim actors subtly or overtly aspired to acknowledge notions of constitutionalism by crafting a distinct political tradition: think of Ahmad Effendi, who unsuccessfully tried to run for the colonial parliament in the 1890s; Abdullah Abdurahman (1872-1940), the leader of the African People's Organisation and renowned Cape Town city councillor between 1910 and 1940; Imam Achmad Cassiem, the Qibla leader, who recently became a city councillor despite his earlier rejection of secular democratic participation; and Ebrahim Rasool, the former Western Cape Premier, who has been a leading political interlocutor for Muslim political participation in a secular democracy.

My account is aimed at showing how Muslims come to terms with the intersection of religion, law, identity and modern social realities in complex ways.

It is a story of how Muslims take on board ideas such as the rule of law, engaging with modern notions of equality and democracy in order to realign these ideas with their views of the sharia (see Moosa 2010).

My examples show this: Abdol Burns's religious and political discourses were shaped in the context of colonial Cape Town and the formation of nascent Muslim communities in colonial space; and the reaction to Imām Haron's radical politics was shaped by the political accommodations and quiescence of Muslims generally during the apartheid years.

The *ʿulamā* bodies of South Africa were reluctant to criticise the system of racial discrimination because their theology preferred stability and conformity, instead of agitation or revolution. Criticism and resistance came from younger generations of students and youths and some religiously trained *ʿulamā*.

These younger Muslims managed to convince some *ʿulamā* to address racial discrimination and political disenfranchisement, but on the whole one could say that the mainstream *ʿulamā* groups were primarily concerned with their class and ethnic interests.

From evidence gleaned from other international contexts, it seems that Muslim minorities have always been mainly concerned with finding some form of accommodation with the hegemonic or dominant interests.

So, it seems as if my normative political position – that is, to understand how Muslims can play a much more critical role in the transformation of their own internal traditions as well as challenging the prevailing corrosive politics of the day – is politically untenable. And a resistance politics and internal reform remain historically unimagined, save for some marginal attempts at critical reforms.

Mawlānā Hendricks's open support for President Zuma in 2008 should be understood in the light of a complex set of discourses that informed and constituted the political and discursive field of the MJC in the post-1994 period.

I would say that Muslim subjectivity – how Muslims go about establishing their discursive responses in a modern secular context – is fashioned out of active and creative engagement with the state and the instruments of governance.

According to Moosa (2010), what is palpable is that these encounters among a variety of discourses – Islamic and non-Islamic – produce new formations of law, self and society.

11. THE *ḤIKMAH* (WISDOM) OF ADVOCATE THULI MADONSELA, PUBLIC PROTECTOR, REPUBLIC OF SOUTH AFRICA[1]

SOCIAL JUSTICE COMMITMENTS FASHIONED IN THE CAULDRON OF THE ANTI-APARTHEID STRUGGLE

Today is our country's 20th annual celebration of Human Rights Day. We have chosen a secular democratic dispensation as the political path by which we build this country into a unified, non-racial, non-sexist dispensation. We have done this in fidelity to addressing our country's legacy of racial exclusion and social closure. Our ethical commitments are informed by the ideals of social justice, inclusion and transformation.

Steve Biko (1946-1977), Solomon Mahlangu (1956-1979), Neil Aggett (1953-1982), Imam Abdullah Haron and many others paid the price of martyrdom as the ultimate expression of their commitment to justice. They were motivated by a social imaginary based on justice and equality for all. It was an imaginary that inspired a broad movement across the length and breadth of our country in order to secure our country's democratic foundations. This, we believe, would provide a platform for achieving human dignity and equality for all.

While apartheid intended to block off human life through racial exclusion, we were able to establish flourishing counter-commitments. People, young and old, of all faith and ideological persuasions, committed themselves to social justice. We refused to be cowered by the limitations that apartheid imposed on our minds, social practices and ethical commitments.

Muslim participation in the struggle was galvanised by the qur'anic injunction in *Ṣūrah al-Qaṣaṣ* (The narration), where Allah (SWT) declares:

> And We wished to be gracious to those who were being oppressed in the land, to make them leaders (in faith) and make them heirs (Q. 28:V5).

The commitments we established during the anti-apartheid years were informed by a radical view of change meant to create the social conditions for human flourishing, especially for the most downtrodden. Our democratic commitments were meant to unleash our human ingenuity and creativity to redress the devastation of apartheid.

THE MESSINESS OF DEMOCRACY

Over the last 20 years, the messiness associated with our country's commitment to a democratic dispensation has been surprising and unexpected. The idea of achieving

1 *Jumu'ah khuṭbah* – Claremont Main Road Masjid, Human Rights Day, 21 March 2014.

an egalitarian society as something inevitable and easily attained simply because we lived by certain high-sounding ideological commitments was very quickly dispelled.

We were brought to the realisation that human rights are a deeply contested terrain. For example, in the Muslim community we still have not, and probably will not in the foreseeable future, achieve recognition for Muslim Family Law under a democratic dispensation. Contestation within the Muslim community meant that we could not find a human rights basis to resolve this matter. Women and children have to endure the worst consequences of an inequitable family law dispensation that is loosely regulated in our communities.

The Truth and Reconciliation Commission was an example of a productive political resolution of this country's striving for reconciliation and truth. But it has struggled to deal adequately with demands by victims for proper recompense. Our country has had to address demands for social transformation at the very same time that reductive economic arrangements worldwide have impacted on the ability of our state to deliver on its social mandate. Trying to ride the tiger of neoliberal capitalism, the macro-economic choices that this country made had a fundamentally reductive impact on our ability to undo the legacy of apartheid.

The consequence is nevertheless a remarkable, yet uneven, set of developmental achievements. We achieved full educational access, but we are struggling to achieve a quality schooling system. We built houses and provided sanitation, but did not secure widespread sustainable living conditions for our country's poor.

Black economic empowerment has seen the emergence of a black business class and a burgeoning middle class who are disconnected geographically and materially from their places of origin.

We witnessed an increase in violence against women, children and the elderly. Our criminal justice system struggles to function optimally, and our policing services are unable to maintain competence and capacity.

In this light, the middle classes have increasingly exercised private options: private and ex-Model C schooling, private health care, and private security services. The overwhelming majority of working-class people have to access public options that provide services of variable quality.

There is an exemplary story to tell about the ability of rights-based social movements such as the Aids activist group, Treatment Action Campaign; the shack dwellers movement, Abahlali baseMjondolo; and the now disestablished HIV activist group, Positive Muslims, to pressure government and communities to become responsive to specific social delivery issues.

This is the uneven state of our country's democracy within which we have to find our human agency, and our individual and collective voices. This is where the Claremont Main Road Masjid (CMRM), with its range of social welfare and development activities, education and literacy campaigns, and interfaith work, among other things, has been exemplary. The mosque is playing a leading role as a Muslim institution in the city. It has moved way beyond the ceremonial, recitation and pietistic culture that has come to dominate Muslim practice in Cape Town.

This culture seemed to have turned inward, to an exclusive focus on the individual and communal 'self,' which has prevented the city's Muslims from making productive outward connections to broader social challenges. In contrast, CMRM has responded over many decades now to the challenge of connecting its internal religious commitments to external commitments to the wider community.

MOVING BEYOND CYNICISM

In response to the chequered and uneven record of delivery during the democratic period, we are aware that cynicism comes very easily. Cynicism might even be justifiable. We can ill afford to develop political stances that cut us loose from the unfolding drama of our country. However, to suggest that we should not adopt a cynical attitude towards our civic participation is not to deny that people have real grievances and even a sense of dread at the directions our country has taken. It is understandable that many have lost hope in our ability to live in a spirit of devotion to progressive and productive commitments.

I would venture to say that the uneven development legacy of the past twenty years is not the main cause of our despair. But it is a contributing factor. I think there is understanding of our country's halting development orientations in the face of a legacy of historical underdevelopment and the difficulty of having to provide infrastructure for all our people.

The despair and disappointment, however, are the outcome of observing what has begun to amount to a culture of corruption in our society, and most importantly in government, the bureaucracy and in the business community where many of the drivers of corruption originate.

These are the very instruments by which our society is meant to deliver on its transformation objectives. Corruption in government and the public and private sectors are deeply troubling and unjust.

There are many hardworking governmental officials and bureaucrats who do important work under difficult conditions. But, as Minister Ebrahim Patel explained in a *khuṭbah* at this mosque about 15 months ago:

> If we allow corruption to become endemic, affecting day-to-day conduct of the business of the state, we create a dysfunctional system in which the state no longer serves the interests of the people, but is simply a means to the accumulation of wealth by a few.

There is now precisely a generalised sense, correct or not, that the depth of corruption in the public sector is endemic and has begun to eat away at the fabric of our constitutional democracy.

Disappointment and cynicism have emerged in the light of the realisation that our capacity to deliver basic human rights is being compromised by corruption. This view has led Imam Rashied Omar, in an *'Īd khuṭbah* in 2012, to exhort that, "We can no longer remain mute in the face of endemic corruption. Our silence and indifference render us accomplices in the crime of corruption. We need to muster the courage to speak out unequivocally and in unison against the growing corruption trend in South Africa".

Imam Rashied is correct; Perhaps we have become mute, voiceless, devoid of agency to act, as he suggests, in the face of corruption. Perhaps we have become indifferent, fearful, lazy or too comfortable.

THE *ḤIKMAH* OF ADVOCATE THULI MADONSELA

I want to suggest that we have recently seen a moral beacon shining brightly in the darkness that accompanies our apathy and indifference.

I am reminded of the *ḥadīth* (saying of Prophet Muhammad) in which Prophet Muhammad (peace be upon him) was reported to have said: "Wisdom is the lost property of the believer. Wherever believers find such wisdom they are most deserving of it" (narrated by al-Tirmidhī).

This *ḥikmah* (wisdom) has presented itself in the person of Advocate Thuli Madonsela and the office of the Public Protector. My view is that we would do well as a community and nation to embrace the *ḥikmah* of the Public Protector.

The office of Public Protector is a constitutionally provided Chapter 9 institution charged with the mission of investigating corruption in government and the public sphere.

Our Constitutional architects deemed it vital for this institution to keep government in check on the assumption that, when bureaucrats and government officials encounter large sums of money in the daily execution of their duties, they would be tempted.

Corruption (*fasād*), bribery (*rishwah*) and nepotism (*wasṭah*) are common occurrences in and around governments the world over.

In 2013 the Public Protector received 37 770 charges of corruption in the public service. This is astonishing, especially since we only get to hear about the high profile cases. What is even more astounding is that the Public Protector's Office was able to finalise 22 400 (60%) of its cases during 2013, with a budget of a meagre R200 million.

Clearly, this is a case where we as civil society have to fight to have this Office strengthened on the basis that our country must be in a position to more effectively address the increase in corruption.

Increasing the Office's effectiveness is in our country's best interest – in *Fiqh* (legal jurisprudential) terms this is regarded as a *maslaḥah* (in service of the public interest).

Under enormous stress created by delays and political stonewalling, insults and abuse, the Office of the Public Protector was able to clearly and without drama or fanfare lift the lid on corruption, irregular tendering, overspending and the general abuse of public money to fund, for example, opulence at the President's Nkandla residence. Based on painstaking work over a four-year period, her Office implicated ministers, bureaucrats, contractors and the President himself.

The Public Protector's work and findings are a *ḥikmah* worth embracing. Allah, the sublime, explains in *Ṣūrah al-Baqarah* (The cow):

> When they are told; 'Do not spread corruption in the land', they respond by saying; 'We are true social reformers'. But in reality they are purveyors of corruption though they realise it not (Q. 2:V11 and V12).

Governments are meant to be the political vehicle for bringing about social reform. However, when (as has happened in the Nkandla case) governance is used as a ruse for fraudulent spending of taxpayers money, then a great *fasād* or ethical misconduct has been committed.

The Public Protector's wisdom is a shining light. She and her Office are inspirational. They have shown the way back to a politics tied to ethical conduct. Her example is an inspiration to us all, an *uswatun ḥasanah* (a good example).

I agree with the Institute for Security Studies, which points out that "The Public Protector's investigation into excessive spending on Nkandla has been an important moment in South Africa's constitutional democracy. It sends a clear signal that where there are allegations of impropriety in public administration, all individuals – regardless of political or socio-economic standing – will be investigated. The purpose is to ensure that every endeavour will be made to protect the interest of the public".

We should be galvanised to recommit ourselves to ethical conduct in our relations and transactions, whether big or small, in our workplaces, our business transactions, and the conduct of our families.

We should support efforts in the legal/constitutional realm to give the Public Protector's Office more teeth so that the consequences of malfeasance are more clearly defined.

We should clamour for a legal provision to prevent a sitting President from determining action in cases in which he or she is implicated.

And we should form part of a lobby to advocate for the expansion of the budget of the Public Protector's Office. Democracy can only be secured if we drastically reduce the levels of endemic poverty in our country. This Office has a crucial role to play in this endeavour.

It is in actively securing our democracy against corruption that we are able to provide a bulwark against indifference and cynicism.

Such activity would lay the basis for reclaiming our country's political imaginary from those who are abusing our democracy. We have to boldly declare that this abuse will not happen in our name.

It is to a politics of engaged democratic citizenship in service of social justice to which we recommit ourselves on this 20th anniversary of Human Rights Day.

12. DISCOVERING THE PURPOSE OF RAMAḌĀN IN THE TIME OF LOAD SHEDDING[1]

Time is a powerful conceptual organiser in Islamic discourse. The Qur'an commands believers to establish concrete righteous practices to give time a productive quality.

I suggest in this chapter that the time we are currently living in is largely out of joint; in other words, we are living in a time of disorientation, which the Qur'an refers to as a state of *khusr* (a state of loss or flight – Q. 94:V1).

LOAD SHEDDING AS TIME OUT OF JOINT

This time out of joint is characterised by people struggling to survive amid precarious economic infrastructure, collapsed labour markets and crumbling social welfare systems.

The majority of our country's poor live from hand to mouth. We see people increasingly trying to make their livelihoods in the informal, illicit and service sectors of our society. Few people have decent jobs with decent wages, medical and pension benefits. Lifestyles are thus precarious and unstable.

This situation manifests itself in increases in disease, ill health and early mortality. Single-parent families and rates of divorce are skyrocketing. An increase in the number of children growing up in broken homes is one tragic outcome of this situation.

It is clear that load shedding has exacerbated this situation. It has, for example, impacted quite dramatically on the sensate experiences of fasting Muslims. Load shedding has changed how and when we prepare our food and organise our daily ritual practice schedules.

Our bodily experience of this year's fast has been affected, for the worse, forcing us to make adaptations to the way we experience our days of *ʿibādah* (acts of worship). In other words, figuratively speaking, as a result of the impact of load shedding, fasting has come to 'taste' different.

My aunt in Mitchells Plain spoke of having to get used to the taste of cold soup and *daltjies*, but quickly adds that "it's Allah's will and we learn to *ṣabr* (persevere)". Her son is less sanguine, murmuring about the horror of a "*pwaasa sonder ligte*" (fasting without electricity).

On the other hand, the Imam in Parkwood speaks about the beauty of sharing a flask of boiling water with his Muslim neighbour for his tea at *ifṭār* (break of fast). And we are encouraged by the *muṣallī* (the mosque congregant) who cautions us to appreciate what we have compared to those less fortunate.

---

1 First published in *Muslim Views*, Ramaḍān, 2015.

Clearly people are not paralysed by their poverty or hardships. They draw on the best of their cultural and religious traditions, community value systems and human connectedness to invent new modes of support, survival and getting by.

'PROPER RECOGNITION' AS A BASIS FOR NON-JUDGEMENTAL MORAL ENGAGEMENT

Times like these require us to step back and allow the 'ground' of people's harsh lives and experiences to speak for themselves. Political brokers, religious leaders and advice-givers would be forced to listen to the pain and suffering of lives lived largely out of sight of formal religious and social institutions.

If we become properly attuned to the acuteness of people's struggles and pain, we would be able to place ourselves in a position to respond with ethical clarity and wise counsel. However, hearing people's pain is only a necessary first step.

We would hear the stories of people all over Cape Town relating their struggles for subsistence and making productive lives. We would understand how the demands of bare survival are now wired into people's material and mental make-up as they struggle to make ends meet.

We would get to understand how hunger and desperation are forcing people to clutch at whatever they can to keep body and soul together. We would also understand why people become involved in the illicit economy, through the sale of illegal goods, drug running and the use of their bodies to make money.

Proper recognition of one's role in mitigating these circumstances requires abandoning the knee-jerk response to moralise about such choices or to judge people who are desperate. Instead, a response of non-judgmentalism would grant us some legitimacy to offer counsel and support.

The question arises as to the meaning of the core lesson of fasting, that is, how we come to understand our connections and commitments to the confounding poverty that characterises our lives and those of the majority in the city?

We would try to understand the small (and large) precarious adaptations that Muslims and other people are now making in the light of having to live in conditions of poverty and collapsing social structures.

What I believe ought to emerge is political and religious ethics that could speak with clarity to our human drama. My deeper issue is with the inability of our political and religious discourses to understand and properly connect with this situation, in effect offering very little by way of direction for ethical living in complex times.

The reorganising impact of load shedding on our sensate experiences – how people experience their daily struggles on their bodies and in their souls – should cause us to pause for reflection. The struggles of ordinary folk to survive poor schooling, food insecurity and rising unemployment and crime should force us to establish practices that ameliorate the plight of struggling folk.

THE SYSTEMIC PROVENANCE OF SOCIAL SUFFERING

These personal experiences, however, have a broader, more systemic, provenance which we ignore at our peril. Load shedding, for example, represents larger fault lines in our body politic.

It is clear that our political system has been deeply affected by neoliberal economic principles. The current government, at all levels, has demonstrably favoured a politics of withdrawal from its commitments to the social welfare and development needs of the citizenry.

The nightmare of Marikana, the corruption of Nkandla and flouting of the Al-Bashir arrest warrant are clear signs of our politicians' unwillingness to legitimise their politics through socially just responses to the plight of the poor.

They are also incontrovertible proof of the current government's lack of commitment to securing a political platform to help poor people mitigate their poverty, let alone providing a platform for promoting social cohesion and stability.

Our neoliberal politics does not just shape public policy. It literally changes us and the world around us in a very physical way. The narratives inherent in this doctrine shape the way we move and care and look and feel. The consequences of neoliberalism are now being written on the bodies of us ordinary people. Depression, anxiety, eating disorders and social isolation are all symptoms of a society crippled from the inside out by declining standards of living.

These, I believe, are the terms and terrain on which religious, civic and other institutions now have to engage their flock. Struggling people do not require dollops of rhetoric and posturing. They require full recognition of their worthwhile lives as they figure out ways of adapting, surviving and even flourishing.

SHARED LOCALISED SOCIAL PRACTICES TO AMELIORATE LIVELIHOODS 'IN JOINT'

Muslims who come to full recognition, through their reflexive practices in Ramaḍān, will commit themselves to activities in their own communities by co-living, sharing and struggle. Our life's activities will be time/space-bound and 'in joint', in other words always productive and shared.

One such example could be a targeted campaign to arrest the early dropping out of young children from school, a trend that is increasing at an alarming rate in townships. As my involvement in one local school community in Cape Town's northern suburbs shows, mitigating school drop-out involves mobilising various community structures including mosques, churches, the local counsellor, police services and social welfare officers to provide safe educational spaces for children.

Helping, for example, with the children's homework, organising sport and having them eat something nourishing would persuade children to invest in their learning. It also means engaging families to support their children's education.

And, crucially, local activism should be brought to bear on the school and governmental structures. This is based on a politics of making the government responsive to people's needs. Where Muslims participate in targeted civic activity, together with others, they will be able to help leverage a more productive governmental response.

This example of creative local co-producing activities could also apply to efforts to obtain a better health and welfare dispensation or more responsive policing in neighbourhoods.

CONCLUSION

The time of load shedding is a time out of joint. It signifies the gap between people's everyday struggles to survive in poor contexts and their collapsing social and economic infrastructure. The survivalist responses of ordinary folk have stepped into the breach, mitigating the worst consequences of impoverished livelihoods.

Ramaḍān places an obligation on Muslims to develop a full connectedness to boosting the quality and nature of our lives in our communities. We would have to recognise the vitality and depth of the survivalist practices of people who struggle to make ends meet.

Recognition and connectedness, however, require a further step; we have to involve ourselves in local practices to secure better living arrangements, through productive practices (*al-aʿmāl al-ṣālihāt*), in community and through co-creation. Such practices would stand a chance of fashioning opportunities for advancing healthy living conditions in our neighbourhoods. As the Qur'an instructs, the productive generation of *viable times in joint* now depends on ordinary people's local practices aimed at securing sustainable livelihoods.

13. CULTIVATING RECOGNITION TO ADVANCE ENVIRONMENTAL JUSTICE[1]

This *khuṭbah* focuses on environmental justice and sustainability in the light of the threat of climate change, global warming, environmental pollution and ecological imbalances all over the world.

These are affecting quality of life, threatening to destroy the very material basis necessary for human existence. We see this in rising temperatures, melting ice caps and rising sea levels.

Humans are being affected on a daily basis with an increase in diseases related to air pollution, and dwindling food resources as a result of desertification of agricultural land and marine resources that are becoming rapidly exhausted.

This issue now confronts us as Muslims as a matter of urgency. We have to persuade ourselves of the need for an appropriate response, based on proper recognition of the nature, depth and extent of the crisis.

This *khuṭbah* is an attempt to lay out the terms of such recognition. I start out with an admission that such recognition will not come easily, and it is my suggestion that we have to confront our ecological fragility at multiple levels.

No one is apparently going to die spectacularly, immediately and directly as a result of global warming. The issue does not seem to conjure enough alarm to get people focused. Unlike incurable diseases such as cancer, HIV and Aids, and even certain strains of tuberculosis, death by environmental pollution and climate change is not imminent.

This lulls us into complacency, and yet the danger is imminent. The best we can say is that our grandchildren will have to survive in the light of earth's diminishing resources in 50 years, all 7 billion or more of them, and that will lead to a scramble for resources that will affect the quality of life for all of the world's people. People like Al Gore make movies such as *An Inconvenient Truth* to scare us out of our complacency, and activists warn us about the impending disaster.

THE NEED FOR URGENCY

But we seem not to understand the urgency, nor are we preparing to radically adapt our lifestyles to mitigate and address the sustainability of the *dunyā'* (this world). My suggestion is thus that most people, communities and nations suffer from a failure to recognise the impending ecological disaster coursing its way into the very fabric of our lives, affecting how we now live and die, the quality of our existence, the scarcity of resources for human survival, where droughts and floods affect our livelihoods, causing famine, forced human migration and wars.

1 *Khuṭbah,* Claremont Main Road Mosque, October 2015.

What then should an Islamic response be in the face of such lack of recognition; what should the terms of our recognition be, and how should we make productive use of our Allah-given human ingenuity in responding to the many dimensions of this crisis?

In other words, once we have recognised the depth and extent of the crisis, how do we get going in addressing this crisis? We have to consider how we establish productive practices (*ʿamāl al-ṣālihāt*), how we engage in Allah's call for us as humans to be his *khalīfatullāhi fi`l- arḍ*, God's vicegerents or human agents for good on this earth.

THINGS ARE OUT OF PLACE (ẒULM)

With regard to recognition (*ma'rifah*), it is clear that something about our existence is profoundly 'out of place'. Human practices in the pursuit of economic gain have over the last 200 years been based on the unbridled exploitation of Allah's earth. Humans seemed to have behaved as if there is to be no *ḥisāb* (accountability), no reckoning with the impact of our behaviour, without any awareness that we will run out of material resources, or undermine ecological sustainability.

Let me illustrate this with an example: almost the whole of the Middle East has been totally immersed in its oil industry for over a hundred years. These countries' entire livelihoods, their economic development, their educational, social and cultural modernisation have been founded on the relentless exploitation of a natural non-renewable resource, a fossil fuel, the production of which gave these countries untold riches and prosperity. But it has also created the world's dirtiest air per square kilometre, leading to many diseases and health challenges.

What is not in place is responsible and forward-looking economic development sensitive to the surrounding ecological systems, clean air technologies, etc. These countries have only now awoken to the impending disaster on their shores, in their water and on their agricultural lands. Food security is a major challenge

Multinational petroleum companies have been deeply complicit in this degeneration. We remind ourselves of the role of BP in the Mexican Gulf last year when an oil leak on a rig led to a massive ecological disaster, not to speak of the horror that ordinary people in countries such as Nigeria and the Niger Delta undergo when oil companies, without a conscience, despoil the environment in the search for oil, or 'black gold' as it has become known.

ẒULM AS HUMAN MALPRACTICE

The Qur'an uses the term '*ẓulm*' or darkness to refer to such human malpractices. This term in exegetical terms means 'to put something out of its rightful place'. '*Ẓulm*' is a reference to the path trodden by people who deny the truth (*ḥaq*) of Allah, and his creation, who through their daily behaviour violate Allah's *mīzān* (or balance). '*Ẓulm*' is a qur'anic concept that captures human beings' complicity in violating Allah's creation, of putting the natural order of things out of alignment, of upsetting the balance.

Such *ẓulm*, or transgression, will incur Allah's wrath. By insisting on transgressive practices, we jeopardise our long-term survival, as in the case of oil pollution for economic gain and material wealth, oblivious to the deleterious impact on the environment.

I would like to suggest that such transgressive human actions are governed by a desire for immediate gratification and not a *taqwa* (God consciousness) based on the long view, the recognition that our behaviour has consequences beyond our lifespan.

An environmentally aware consciousness, *taqwa*, now requires that we cultivate the ability to recognise the impact of our behaviour well into the future and cultivate the necessary capacity to adjust our behaviour accordingly. In *Ṣūrah al-Zumar* (The Groups) [Q. 39:V53], Allah, the Sublime, offers one of the key ways of laying the basis for responding to this human-induced '*ẓulm*'. Allah declares:

> Say: "O my Servants who have transgressed against their souls! Despair not of the Mercy of Allah. For Allah forgives all sins: for He is Oft-Forgiving, Most Merciful".

The emphasis in this *āyāt* (verse) is on recognising one's 'transgression against one's own soul, against one's own being, one's own existence', whether this is a recognition of one's transgression against one's body when one overeats, breaking traffic rules and putting oneself in danger, recognising one's transgression against one's partner, children, fellow workers, or neighbour for not honouring them as people with their own rights over us.

We transgress our own *nafs* (soul) in our consumption choices, in acquiring fuel-guzzling cars, overspending on weekly groceries, and the failure to cut down on our electricity use. More broadly, as a nation, we transgress our *nafs* when we do not use cheaper, cleaner energy sources, when we do not become a nation that recycles garbage, or conserves water, or promotes hardy indigenous plants that do not need much water.

At the smaller, individual and communal level, we transgress against our *nafs* when we provide too much food at our *gaajats* (liturgies), our seventh, fortieth and hundredth commemorations of our dead. We transgress when we load our food with fat and sugar, and when we are unable to change our diets to mitigate the common diseases among us such as diabetes, high cholesterol levels and heart failure. And we transgress, committing what the *fiqh* (legal jurisprudence) calls a '*makrūh*' (an abominable and disapproved act) when we are unable to address our addiction to smoking, causing illnesses such as lung cancer and emphysema, which are an enormous drain on our health system.

REDRESSING OUR TRANSGRESSIONS

The Qur'an's view is that it is only when we redress these transgressions, big and small, that we place ourselves in the position to obtain Allah's *raḥmah*, his infinite mercy. We then place ourselves in a position to address our myriad environmental and ecological challenges to restore the balance through our human conduct, based on environmentally aware *taqwa* or God consciousness.

We would then be able to restore the natural balance established by Allah, who declares in the holy Qur'an in *Ṣūrah Āli-ʿImrān* (The Family of Imran, Q. 3:V190-1):

> Behold! in the creation of the heavens and the earth, and the alternation of night and day – there are indeed Signs for people of understanding who celebrate the praises of God, standing, sitting, and lying down on their sides, and contemplate the (wonders of) creation in the heavens and the earth (with the thought): Our Lord! not for nothing have You created (all) this! Glory be to You! Grant us salvation from the torment of fire.

Let me end off with a comment on the importance of water in Islam, which emphasises the importance of a responsible and responsive approach to our environment and our contemporary challenges to restore an ecological balance and to establish sustainable livelihoods. A beautiful *ḥadīth* (saying of Prophet Muhammad) recorded in Ibn Mājah, emphasises this environmental consciousness: Prophet Muhammad (peace be upon him) passed by his companion Sa`ad, who was performing his *wuḍū* (ablutions) and said:

> "What is this wastage, O Sa`ad?"
>
> "Is there wastage even in (such a sacred act as) washing for prayer?" asked Sa`ad; and he (the Prophet) said, "Yes, even if you are by a flowing river!"

In a few words Muhammad (peace be upon him) provided a fundamental principle regarding environmental sustainability. That is, even if we supposedly have abundance, we are forbidden to waste resources. Water, of course plays an enormous part in human existence. The Qur'an affirms this when Allah declares in *Sūrah al-Anbiyā'* (The Prophets, Q. 21:V30): "We made from water every living thing".

Water is so much more important in an arid desert context, where the early Muslims under Muhammad (peace be upon him) made their way in establishing Allah's *tawḥīd* (unicity). The early Muslims must have had an acute understanding of the limitations of their geography, the impact of desert conditions and the scarcity of water on their functioning as a community. No wonder that control over an oasis or well was such an important consideration.

The early Muslims' survival in the face of human, material and ecological adversity is a source of deep inspiration for present-day sustainable living. It provides a principled platform to guide us in our 21st-century quest for sustainable living in the light of our ecological challenges in a world fast running out of its ability to sustain its growing population.

14. LIVING IN FIDELITY TO THE CONSTITUTION[1]

During the 1990s we as a country chose to regulate state governance, institution building and human relationships (*muʿāmalāt*) on the basis of a constitutional democracy. We succeeded in creating a constitutional platform, however imperfect, as a means of working toward becoming a common nation and shared citizenship. People from diverse backgrounds reconciled themselves to living in an inclusive and just society.

We struggled as a nation with the deep and ugly divisions of the past. We committed ourselves as citizens to working towards a future based on equality, fairness and the rule of law. This was founded on a promise that a path of reconciliation (*ṣulḥ*) would secure the inclusion of all in our democratic polity and the rebuilding of our country.

In Islamic terms, this position is based on the much quoted *ḥadīth* in which prophet Muhammad (peace be upon him) was reported to have explained that a Muslim's way of life is based on sound and productive human relations. Establishing productive human relations and practices in search of the common good is the defining feature of becoming fully human.

Our constitutional democratic commitments were based on a promissory note: that democracy would provide us with the tools and material foundations to struggle for, and secure, a better life for all. Our patient commitment (*ṣabr*) to a fair and inclusive country was based on the realisation that change would be complex and difficult.

The Constitution provided a basis for optimal inclusion, a place in the sun for all. Our constitutional dispensation was acceptable because it was founded on the necessity of actively conferring human dignity on the people of this country. It passed the qur'anic test of dignity, honour and equal worth as one of the key organising principles of Islam. Allah (SWT) declares in *Ṣūrah al-Iṣrā* (The Night Journey, Q. 17:V70):

> Now, indeed, We have conferred dignity on the children of Adam, and dispersed them over land and sea, provided for them sustenance out of the good things of life, and favoured them far above most of our Creation.

This *āyah* (verse) establishes the raison d'être of the Islamic ethos for living worthy lives: equality among people irrespective of race, class, gender, sexuality, nationality and geographic origin.

These values were enshrined in South Africa's Constitution. And, as Muslims, we walked with other communities a contested, noisy and complex path towards reclaiming our dignity. A consensus emerged among different faith and ideological groupings about the rules of the game as laid out in the Constitution: the rule of

1 *Khuṭbah,* Claremont Main Road Mosque, 22 April 2016.

law, a commitment to counter corruption and ensure the equitable provision of social services.

Our democracy allows contestation over the meaning and distribution of rights such as the right to housing, education and health. In the public domain we have seen protests on the street, strikes in the workplace, and policy contestation in think tanks and lobbies, parliament, the media and in the various courts of our land.

Rights-bearing citizens have been using the instruments of our democracy to stake their claim for recognition. Poor policy choices in education, health, housing, policing, economic and industrial policy were severely contested. Many communities and organisations started organising around social welfare objectives such as quality schooling, the extension of grants, housing provision, and health systems improvement.

South Africa is a vibrant, noisy and fractious democracy. And while the provision of viable livelihoods has been uneven, citizens at least have some skin in the political game. It is the promissory note of our democracy, the ideals of justice and equality, that keeps us in this contested political game.

One lesson has been that powerful people, financially and organisationally, are the most visible and their opinions and policy preferences are taken seriously. People from older and newer privileged contexts make disproportionate demands on our polity and enjoy enormous privilege.

We have also learnt that those who resist, organise and push for their rights, are able to leverage responsiveness from the state. Those who do not organise are invisible to the political powers that be. They are ignored and continue to suffer the daily indignities associated with poverty and inequality.

The promise of our democracy remains wrapped up in the possibility of leveraging a type of politics at local, municipal, regional and national level that will render the state responsive to the demand for worthwhile livelihoods.

THE PERILS OF INFIDELITY TO THE CONSTITUTION

Our constitutional democracy is brought into question when our country fails to deliver on the promise of a fairer society. A democracy's legitimacy is only secured when a country is able to deliver on people's legitimate expectations. Defending the Constitution is therefore a defence of an inclusive and productive path towards securing sustainable livelihoods.

We keep ourselves in the democratic game only to the extent to which we are able to concretise the egalitarian vision of our democracy. It is in this light that we have to question two of the biggest infractions of our present-day politics: one is the flouting of the Constitution by the President in the light of the Nkandla debacle, and the other is the capture of the state by family interests.

The Nkandla debacle is part of a steady pattern of corruption and looting of the state's resources over many years. The Nkandla matter brought corruption, tenderpreneurship and the impunity of patronage politics into the spotlight. Nkandla confirmed government corruption as a pivot of state functioning.

The blatant capture of the state by one family follows on from the history of state capture by the apartheid state: the state follows the same pattern of an oligarchy operating only for the benefit of those who have access to patronage networks. The outcome is the same: under apartheid corruption and state capture served as a proxy for white advancement. Current patronage politics serve to buttress the enrichment of the politically connected nouveau riche.

In a *khutbah* that I presented in this mosque in March 2014, I called for embracing the Public Protector's report on the Nkandla renovations in the light of the Head of State's ethical misconduct in spending public funds on the renovations.

The Public Protector's findings were a *ḥikmah* worth embracing. About corruption and its purveyors, Allah, the sublime, explains in *Sūrah al-Baqarah (*The cow, V11 and V12):

> When they are told; 'Do not spread corruption in the land', they respond by saying; 'We are true social reformers'. But in reality they are purveyors of corruption though they realise it not.

This mosque came out with an unequivocal statement hailing the Public Protector's report, urging "our government to comply with the recommendations of the report" (CMRM statement, 23 March 2014).

The Public Protector's report and recommendations were borne out by the recent Constitutional Court's pronouncement against the President, who chose to challenge the 'implementability' of her recommendations. The Court ruled that the President was in violation of the Constitution when he refused to implement the Public Protector's recommendations to repay a portion of the money for extending his home.

The Court also found the National Assembly, our parliament, in violation of the Constitution when it chose to ignore the recommendations. The National Assembly erroneously established a subcommittee of parliament to consider the report. Similarly, the Minister of Police produced a report stating that the Constitutional Court ruling had no legal standing. In other words, instruments of the state – parliament, various committees and ministries – were abused in an attempt to undermine and invalidate the Public Protector's recommendations.

In the process a core constitutional principle was violated, which is the separation of powers between government as the executive arm of government policy, on the one hand, and the parliament as the legislative arm and overseer of the executive on the other.

Constitutionally, these two arms of state must function independently. Alarmingly, this functional independence was violated in defence of the President; parliament was used to produce an unconstitutional outcome, i.e. absolving the President of guilt. It was left to the third arm of the state, the judiciary, to assert the supremacy of the Constitution. The Constitutional Court instructed the President to adhere to the stipulation of the Public Protector's report, in other words, to pay back the money.

MU'ĀMALĀT (PRODUCTIVE RELATIONS) AS THE ROAD TO OUR HUMAN COMMITMENTS

While we heaved a collective sigh of relief at the clarity provided by the Constitutional Court's judgement, we must ask where this entire episode leaves our country. We have to consider where the impact of corruption, abuse of state resources, and the violation of the Constitution leave us as citizens.

There is no denying that people experienced this moment as deeply disorientating. Combined with rising crime, violence and fear, people choose to withdraw from the public sphere. People understandably tend to become anxious and inward looking under such circumstances. When we observe the government acting against the country's interests, we as ordinary citizens opt to defend those closest to ourselves, providing for our own families, protecting our children and possessions. In such a context broader commitments to good neighbourliness, common courtesy and sharing begin to fritter away. People withdraw behind closed doors to protect themselves against rampant crime on the streets and the violence in our communities.

When the first citizen of the country is seen as flouting the Constitution, we become cynical about the very democracy that we live in. State corruption and patronage are read as signs of an uncaring state. And people have been making tenuous livelihoods in spite of, or in the absence of, a functioning state. Life is lived in twilight zones of poverty, hardship, and single-parent and child-headed households. People have to fend for themselves. They establish moral codes by which they figure out what is important, who should be respected, how cash is distributed, how relationships work, who should go to school or drop out, and who should eat.

It is clear that our chosen democratic path has been rendered ineffectual. State corruption and capture are symbolic of the way the democratic path has been compromised. And people are not stupid. They figure out very quickly how to step into the breach, how to go on with their lives. We as Muslims (and other communities) must now ask how we must intervene in this human drama. Going with the flow or opting out are not options.

The Prophet's advice to engage in *mu'āmalāt* (productive human relations) must take centre stage. Inserting exemplary practices (*'amāl al-ṣālihāt*) into the body politic is crucial. We must continue to emphasise positive relationships in our workplaces and educational institutions.

Our work colleagues, fellow students and friends are deserving of empathy, respect and decency. Advancing their aspirations is as important as being concerned about our own.

Getting involved in social welfare-oriented work takes our *mu'āmalāt* to the next level. Spending part of our wealth in the service of others builds fellowship. It also alleviates hardship and suffering.

Getting involved in social-justice-oriented work, whether in the delivery of better health services or educational opportunities, targets improvement of life circumstances.

The Prophet's advice is now more important than ever: social relations are the terrain of our commitment to common moral values through our civic activities. Our survival as communities depends on our generosity at the very moment when our political leaders look the other way.

The state might have left the game, yet we have no choice but to remain in the game. And part of remaining in the game is to claim a space to exercise our commitment to our democracy on our own terms.

This means participating in the type of politics that can force governmental accountability. We have to bring an accountable and responsive government back into the game through an assertion of common values and practices.

Our humanity depends on remaining in the game of human engagement, interaction and relationships based on beauty, patience, goodness and virtue.

15. FROM RESPONDING TO THE WATER CRISIS TO ACTIVELY ADDRESSING POVERTY AND HARDSHIP[1]

> O You who have attained to faith! When the call to prayer is sounded on the day of congregation, hasten to the remembrance of God, and leave all worldly commerce: this is for your own good, if you but knew it. (*Sūrah al-Jumuʿah,* The Congregation, Q. 62:V9)

This *āyah* (verse) on the imperative of *yawm al-jumuʿah* (the day of congregational prayer) emphasises the need for us humans to come to rest, engage in personal contemplation and congregational prayer.

The *jumuʿah* is a time of submission to individual spiritual connection to Allah, and one's co-existence with others in this world. The *waqt* (time) of *jumuʿah* is also a momentary pause from the challenges and afflictions of our daily life.

Jumuʿah is a time when we are at one with Allah and higher moral purposes, where we reset or recharge our commitments to goodness and fellowship. This is a time when, as the Qur'an explains, the 'heart is at peace', as Allah declares in *Sūrah al-Shuʿarā* (The poets, Q. 26:V89) – "when he will only be happy when he comes before Allah with a peaceful heart".

This is a time when we figure out how to approach Allah with a heart free of evil, with a sound heart, not only in the last moments of life, as the Qur'an exhorts in this *āyah,* but also when one becomes aligned with life's moral purposes.

It is in moments such as our weekly congregational prayer that we are able to perceive clearly how we ought to live in the world, what our priorities are, and how we have to commit to a productive life in pursuit of peace and tranquillity. These moments offer an opportunity to develop and align ourselves with human practices that are responsive to eradicating need, difficulty and hardship.

In this city we have been alerted to this moral purpose in our confrontation with one of the worst droughts to hit the city in living memory. Staring a water crisis in the face forced us to focus on our bare existence – how to make do without water as the most important resource for our survival. At its most basic level the crisis confronts us with our personal water consumption for making food, washing and even brushing our teeth.

Water, of course, plays an enormous part in our existence. The Qur'an affirms this when Allah declares in *Sūrah al-Anbiyā'* (The Prophets, Q. 21:V30): "We made from water every living thing".

A beautiful *ḥadīth* recorded in Ibn Mājah, emphasises a heightened water consciousness in Islam: It was reported that the Prophet Muhammad (peace be upon

1 *Khuṭbah,* Claremont Main Road Mosque, 24 February 2017.

him) passed by his companion Sa`ad, who was performing his *wudu'* (ablutions), and said:

> "What is this wastage, O Sa`ad?"
>
> "Is there wastage even in (such a sacred act as) washing for prayer?" asked Sa`ad; and he (the Prophet) said, "Yes, even if you are by a flowing river!"

In a few words Muhammad (peace be upon him) illustrated a fundamental principle regarding water and environmental sustainability, that is, even if we supposedly have abundance, we are forbidden to waste resources.

But we do not have abundance. The water scarcity forced us to respond to this fact with urgency. As citizens of the city, we have been making the following simple *du`ā* (supplication): O Allah, send us rain.

The words of this prayer reverberate in our physical bodies, eliciting a response. Beseeching Allah for rain has accompanied our adaptation to the urgency of the crisis. It is clear that we are using much less water for our daily living. Mosques and our other social institutions have begun to limit their water consumption considerably, and we have curtailed water use for our ablutions.

It has recently emerged that many businesses, hotels and industries are not complying with the water restrictions, incurring fines instead. If you are an employee in one of these non-complying industries, I want to urge you to pressurise those in your work environment to comply.

It is nonetheless in the face of adversity associated with the drought that ordinary people and communities have come to adapt to the practical imperative for drastic water reduction based on a simple and acute sense of moral and practical necessity.

It has in the process brought families, neighbours, religious leaders and other groups of people together, and opened us up to the possibility of fellowship and cooperation, as encouraged in the Qur'an (*Sūrah al-Mā'idah,* The Table Spread, Q. 5:V6), where Allah exhorts us to "help one another in furthering virtue and God-consciousness, and do not help one another in furthering evil and enmity".

The lesson here is that cooperation, when addressing a disaster (*muṣībah*), or in response to a need, provides us with a greater chance to redress our circumstances positively.

The water crisis highlights a larger issue. While we have become alert to the centrality of water in our lives, we also have to properly understand and engage the human causes of the abnormal weather patterns globally. Climate change and global warming are incontrovertible scientifically proven realities. The earth is getting warmer at an exponential rate. If we do not change our consumption patterns, invest in science to discover and harvest clean energies, oppose nuclear energy and fracking, and develop technologies that can replace our reliance on coal and fossil fuel, we will destroy the ecological sustainability of this planet.

The sparing and wise use of water in the city ought to spur us towards greater awareness of our longer-term ecological sustainability. The poor on this earth and in our city will continue to bear the brunt of our ecological destruction.

The cooperation (*ta`āwun*) required to address this crisis will have to take the form of working with all human communities, with all our intellectual might and cutting-edge research.

We cannot keep on behaving with a short-term consciousness, oblivious to the longer-term human-made calamity that threatens our existence on the planet. But this requires more than our vigilance in addressing our current cycle of periodic droughts.

This requires us to develop a type of *īmān* or consciousness, and activism or *`amāl al-ṣālihāt* (righteous deeds) that connect our spiritual commitments to a life in service to Allah, to the larger moral purpose of creating the conditions for sustainable livelihoods.

Belief in Allah disconnected from a social purpose can so easily lead to an empty and narrow religious formalism. Allah warns in *Sūrah al-Mā`ūn* (the Small Kindnesses) about this disconnect, when Allah asks: "Hast though ever considered [the kind of person] who gives the lie to all moral law?" (Q. 107:V1).

The appropriate qur'anic response is to connect our personal belief and *'ibādah* (acts of worship) to the needs of the orphan, the needy and the refugee.

Our *'ibādah* must of necessity be a platform for making broader commitments to the earth's sustainability and our common human survival.

The Qur'an encourages us to be responsive to large-scale social changes. Allah declares in *Sūrah al-Baqarah* (The cow) (Q. 2:V155):

> And most certainly shall We test you by means of **danger**, and **hunger**, and **loss of wealth**, **of lives** and of **[labour's] fruits**. But give glad tidings unto those who are patient in adversity.

This is a crucial verse. It speaks to a number of major issues that afflict the human condition. This emphasis here is on how situations change, sometimes rapidly, and how these changes throw our livelihoods completely out of whack, putting our very survival as communities and a species under the spotlight. We are required to respond to:

- **danger** associated with changing weather patterns, crime and violence;
- **hunger** associated with poverty and inequality as experienced by more than 50% of the city's inhabitants in its townships and growing informal settlements;
- the changing socio-economic status associated with unemployment, **loss of income and wealth**;
- and the displacement and suffering experienced by refugees when they **search for a stable life in foreign circumstances**.

Positing these as a test, a trial or a challenge to human survival, Allah (SWT) exhorts us to display patience and forbearance in the face of adversity.

Ṣabr, patience in adversity, requires a human commitment that takes us out of our comfort zones. What is required in addressing these crises are personal commitment, strategic intent and unity in purpose and action. What is not productive is racist and xenophobic behaviour, narcissistic politics, protectionism and closing of borders.

An acutely moral response is founded on a disposition of radical hospitality, the idea that we have to sacrifice part of our own comfort to ensure the solace and comfort of others. This is not easy, but this is what is now required of us.

We are required to respond. This is a *farḍ kifāyah* (a collective community responsibility), whether we participate in meeting the welfare needs of our neighbours, provide blankets and food for displaced refugees who are victims of xenophobic attacks, participate in local activism in the areas of social housing in the city, support schools to educate their children, provide safe health infrastructure for the disabled and psychiatrically afflicted, or organise in the workplace against exploitative conditions.

The Qur'an requires us to develop a wide range of responses to address these challenges, and getting involved in one or more of them is now regarded as a recommended practice (*mustaḥab*). Herein lies the glad tidings that Allah promises in the *āyāt* (verse) that I mentioned above: the glad tidings that would come to those who are patient, active and constructively engaged in radical hospitality towards ourselves and others in times of adversity.

I end by making a plea for focusing on the task at hand, not sideshows, or things that will demoralise us. My point of departure is that we have to develop a maturity about first principles. The Qur'an requires nothing less. Eradicating poverty, disease and hardship is the primary organising frame emphasised in the Qur'an.

Managing our affairs in such a way that we honour our commitment to Allah is paramount. We simply have to, as a community, do better to manage our affairs in such a way that we do not become distracted. Strife among families, groups and communities must be managed in a constructive and productive way.

We must avoid the temptation of engaging in petty sectarian battles or unnecessary destructive discourses that drain away the oxygen we need to focus on poverty alleviation and compassionate action. The skirmishes between Ḥanafis and Shāfis, open and closed mosques, Sunnis and Shi`as, and Sufis and Wahhabis, arise from a simple-minded immaturity.

These doctrinal or sectarian struggles are borne of a propensity for *fitnah* (internecine strife), with reference to the use of words, language and deeds to deny people the right to believe. The early Muslims were the victim of the *fitnah* that the disbelievers visited on them, which led to hostility, expulsion and even death.

The Qur'an suggests that a condition of *fitnah* poses a threat to society's normal order in the *āyah* (*Sūrah al-Baqara*h, The Cow, Q. 2:V191), "and tumult and oppression (*fitnah*) are worse than killing." Sectarian skirmishes concentrate on the symptoms of difficult situations, not their causes. The requirement is to identify the causes of our hardships and develop strategic action in response. Sectarianism prevents us from focusing on those issues that matter to communities and it is the call of this *khuṭbah* to develop such a strategic discipline and focus.

Addressing the plight of communities in a world out whack along a number of axes requires wisdom, non-judgmentalism, the exercise of one's intellect, and commitment to address the plight of our communities.

We must aim to establish practices that alleviate the pain of those who suffer from having to live undignified lives and to confer dignity on all God's children through patience and perseverance. And, as Allah declares in *Sūrah al-Iṣrā* (The Night Journey, Q. 17:V70):

> And, now, We (Allah) have indeed conferred dignity on all the children of Adam.

Conferring *karāmah* or dignity on all of Allah's creation is the primary organising frame of human existence, and it is to this pristine cause that we should now commit ourselves with clarity and unwavering purpose.

16. MY IRAN TRIP REVEALS CULTURAL COMPLEXITIES: IMPRESSIONS OF THE COUNTRY AND ITS PEOPLE[1]

We have just returned from a visit to Iran. We visited three cities, spent time with ordinary folk, drove from city to city, participated in two lovely conferences, and saw lots of museums, markets and the country's beautiful landscapes.

We got to understand how this rich and enduring culture is the result of adding onto, never throwing out, their various layers of cultural inheritance, including Persian, Zoroastrian, Islamic, Safavid, (Shah) Pahlavian, socialist, nationalist and various other aspects.

We were also exposed to various elements of the global consumer culture which we observed among young people. We spoke to many young people who taught us about their musical tastes, their love for Western and non-Western movies (which they download from the internet), fashion, clothing, their experiences with the world of work, and desire for travel.

We also got to understand a little bit about how the contradictions between Iran's rich and overlapping cultural inheritances are mediated by the current Islamist emphasis on a particular religious-political articulation.

Some of these mediations are positive and productive, as shown by the country's economic and political self-reliance, and its generally anti-imperial global political stance. Other mediations of the dominant Islamist political sphere seem to be constrained by the lack of opportunity for creativity and innovation, allegations of corruption, and constraints experienced in the areas of gender and class disparity and open political expression.

I got the sense that ordinary folk have found interesting ways of establishing small freedoms in this context, in the way they dress (only a small number of women follow the strict dress code; most chose to wear a small colourful headscarf, make-up and the latest fashions), their adherence to their Persian history (one young female academic explained that she left the 'religion of the mullahs' behind and embraced her Persian identity in flexible ways), and their love of music and dance (done undercover and out of sight).

And some expressed a desire for a more egalitarian society in the areas of gender, criticism of elite domination, and calls for the adoption of minority rights and greater inclusion.

Iran has many minorities, especially in regions that are contiguous to other countries, such as the Kurds, Arabs, Persian Armenians, Lurs, Mazandaranis, Turkmen and religious minorities such as Jews, Christians and Bahais, some of whom have reported being persecuted.

---

1 Published in Al-Qalam, December 2017.

The religious culture is dominated by the Shi`a version of Islam. This means that the country's formal public culture and semiotics are inflected by Shi`a symbolism and religious practices.

What I found interesting, though, and probably in need of greater understanding, was that there was an absence of doctrinal rancour or polemics – in other words, no Sunni-Shi`a polemics, or Sunni vilification. This is instructive for people living in other contexts such as South Africa, and elsewhere, which have seen an increase in anti-Shi`a intolerance over the last five years.

Such intolerance is born of a larger geo-political battle in the Middle East between Saudi Arabia and Iran over expanding their respective spheres of dominance in countries such as Yemen, Lebanon, Iraq and Syria. In this situation, the Shi`a-Sunni polemics is a proxy for geopolitical contestation. Such polemics are clearly a manifestation of long-standing doctrinal disputation, mostly resolved, but now being mobilised in the service of political expansionism.

Iranians get very worked up, almost to a person, by the Wahhabi *takfīri* creed, which is a strain of Islamic discourse that declares every other Islamic discourse anathema. I asked myself whether this reveals an anti-Sunni perspective? Perhaps, I thought. But not from what I could discern. Iranians had an entirely political reading of *takfīri* doctrine; they mention American influence in the Middle East, they were vehemently opposed to the austere literalist interpretation employed by the *takfīris* (those who declare that Muslims of other doctrinal orientations are disbelievers), and there is a geo-political dimension to their opinions, including their views on Saudi influence and expansionism in the Middle East.

Of course, Iran's support for groups in Lebanon, Syria and Yemen makes the country at the very least complicit as a player in ongoing sectarian politics and militarism in the Middle East. One has to ask the question whether their involvement in Middle Eastern conflicts is undertaken for better or worse for the region.

What is clear among all Iranians is that an anti-Israel position is a pillar of political faith, based on a very careful distinction between Zionism as the putative enemy of the region and Judaism as a proud and accepted Abrahamic religion.

I participated in three sessions at two conferences in the cities of Khorramabad and Isfahan: presenting two papers and one four-hour workshop. The latter focused on 'pluralities of knowledges in educational policy and practice'. The workshop elicited exceptionally sharp, critical questions and views which I found surprising. The Irianian participants wanted to know how their educational discourses could be pluralised in a context of such religious discursive dominance, and how to press beyond the limits imposed by such restrictions.

The connections we made were productive and thoughtful. We are pursuing the possibility of a university link with Isfahan University in the city of Isfahan, which is the cultural capital of Iran. This is one of Iran's best universities, with 13 faculties, located on a beautiful campus, in a lovely part of the city.

And, of course, we visited Tehran. The capital city was an amazing mix of architecture, congestion, mad driving, vibrant culture, and people going about their business, making viable lives. This was an important trip, life-affirming in an exciting, astonishing, productive and beautiful way.

Ordinary Iranians have worked out how to 'stand on' many different points of meaning and contradiction, giving expression to their humanness in the softest, gentlest and humblest ways imaginable.

My impressions are indeed perfunctory, based on a short and superficial, yet quite intense, trip. What we observed and experienced gave us a wonderful sense of everyday Iranians and their dignified lives.

17. RESPONDING TO THE DECOLONISATION IMPERATIVE: IMAGINING ISLAM FROM THE PERSPECTIVE OF THE 'WRETCHED OF THE EARTH'[1]

This *khuṭbah* offers an Islamic perspective in response to the call for decolonisation made by students at our country's universities.

Decolonisation calls for an awareness of complex contradictions in our country and directs our attention to the demands of the poor for dignified living.

It points up the ongoing legacy of colonialism and coloniality, and the humiliation that accompanies living in a world of colonial symbols, languages, images, texts, knowledge and practices.

I ask the following: What is a decolonial Islamic approach, and how could such an approach empower marginalised communities to establish productive and viable lives?

A decolonial approach places the downtrodden at the centre of its imagination, not the interests of elites and the powerful. It acknowledges the struggles of slave girls who were forced to work in the master's kitchen, and the labouring men and women who worked on farms and built Cape Town's infrastructure, and were subjected to abuse, torture and sexual violence.

A decolonial Islamic approach focuses on the everyday practices of these men and women who went about establishing viable lives on the edges of the colonial city; who built educational, social welfare and religious practices and institutions despite severe limitations.

Muslims in Cape Town adopted religious and spiritual practices that secured their survival and adaptation. Imbued with a spirit of resistance, they vigorously practised their Sufi liturgies to strengthen their spiritual selves.

They adopted complex literacy practices as can be seen by their *kutub* (religious texts) and handwritten texts in the Jawi-Arabic script, passed on through generations, giving rise to the first written Afrikaans as it was spoken among Cape Town's slave communities.

Their *khalīfah* / *rātib* displays based on body piercing accompanied by rhythmic *dhikr* (liturgies) chanting performances, regarded today by many as a *bid`ah* (innovation), were aimed at showing strength and confusing the colonial order.

Their cultural practices such as the *mawlid* (birthday) celebrations in remembrance of the Prophet Muhammad's (peace be upon him) birth, name-giving ceremonies, and various rites of passage-related activities have been the cornerstones of Muslim community life.

---

1 *Khuṭbah* presented at Claremont Main Road Mosque, 19 January 2018.

The colonial order placed them in positions of wretchedness and subordination, and yet they employed their own rituals, literacies, knowledges and practices to establish viable, yet largely unacknowledged, lives.

Colonial oppression finds an analogy in the Qur'an's depiction of Pharaoh's oppression of his own people. Allah declares in *Sūrah al-Qaṣaṣ* (The narration):

> Behold, Pharaoh exalted himself in the land and divided its people into castes. One group of them he deemed utterly low; he would slaughter their sons and spare (only) their women: for, behold, he was one of those who spread corruption [on earth] (Q. 28:V4).

Pharaoh visited violence and death on those he deemed as being from the lower echelons of society. He killed their male children for fear that they would rebel, and he visited unbounded tyranny on them.

But Allah promises in the next verse that the oppressed shall be liberated from Pharaoh's tyranny and inherit the earth. Allah, the sublime, declares:

> But it was Our will to bestow Our favour upon those [very people] who were deemed [so] utterly low in the land, and to make them forerunners in faith, and to make them heirs (Q. 28:V5).

It is these and other verses of the Quran, and supported by the history and practices that constituted Muhammad's (peace be upon him) prophetic message, that established the focal point of Islam's ethical vision: the downtrodden, the weak and oppressed at the heart of Islam.

Social justice is what ought to be at the centre of our practices, as the Qur'an declares in *Sūrah al-Māidah* (The Table Spread, Q. 5:V8): "Be just: this is closest to being God-conscious".

Prophet Muhammad's (peace be upon him) message emphasised fairness and socially just lives, which threatened to upend the power and privilege of various elites. The early Makkan Muslims were met with hostility and persecution.

The Qur'an's emphasis on justice and fairness is crystal clear: it zooms in on the power relations that sustain poverty and inequality, and it seeks to dismantle them in favour of a fair, just and inclusive dispensation.

We have to apply these ethical dimensions to contemporary life. Bringing the figure of the oppressed or wretched of the earth into full view is a necessary condition for our politics and practices.

We have to ask who the oppressed, the weak and the marginalised in our societies are. And we have to work hard to recognise the complexity of the lives of the downtrodden.

Marginality is a majority experience in Cape Town, but marginal people remain largely hidden from view, from the language of politicians, and from the incredibly exclusionary economic structures of society. The plight of the poor, weak and differently-abled remains hidden from view.

I offer you two examples of how exclusionary discourse work among us in the city of Cape Town. First, Cape Town has a vibrant carnival culture. Around the celebration of the New Year, and in commemoration of freeing the slaves in 1834, the Christmas choirs, minstrels and Malay choirs take to the streets, dressed in carnival regalia, singing and marching through the streets of Cape Town.

The carnivals are an exuberant expression of joy and a symbolic take-over of the city. They have been a feature of Cape Town life for almost two centuries, making a renewed comeback during the last 15 years, as more and more youngsters become involved in the carnival.

The participating groups are organised all over Cape Town's poorer townships, in areas with enormous developmental and social welfare challenges, where schooling has largely broken down, and where a rise in school drop-out rates in lower grades is the order of the day.

What the minstrel and Malay choir culture does is provide a creative outlet for young people, where they learn to socialise among themselves, build friendships and express themselves.

It is these and other cultural markers that allow our communities to retain a sense of cohesiveness in the face of collapsing social and physical infrastructures. This is a case of the wretched of the earth who, left without support, go on to invent community cultural practices to buffer their desperate lives in hard times.

It is, however, no exaggeration to say that many elites among us frown upon these displays of bodily exuberance. There is a trope of respectability and distinction, especially among the upper classes, that is marked by a disdain for the carnivals.

However, such a condescending perspective is borne of a larger marginalisation, which is that the lives of the wretched are never brought into view as worthy of dignity through the provision of good housing, proper education and healthcare.

We may indeed quote from the Qur'an that Allah has dignified the lives of all humans, but disdainful dismissal of the poor serves to distance those respectability-chasing elites from the struggles of the poor.

This attitude segues into a middle class dominated by a politics that prevents the city from making social justice commitments to poor people, who simply become voting fodder to serve the interests of the powerful who live in other parts of the city.

The second example has a long history in Cape Town; it is what I call the 'community to prison complex,' something I observed from my time as a teacher on the Cape Flats. It involves children from broken families, often living off welfare, and going to school intermittently, drawn into the criminal justice system, and basically moving in and out of prison during their childhood and young adult life.

They operate within the illicit economy, selling drugs and getting involved in petty crimes. They are sucked into prison gangs, from which it is almost impossible to escape.

The rise in the incarceration of boys and girls during the last decade has been earth-shattering. This is attributed to the exponential increase in the use of *tik* (methamphetamine), brought on by the collapse of family life, the lure of the criminal economy, the use of their bodies to earn easy money.

According to reports, Pollsmoor prison looks like 'Makkah in Ramaḍān', in reference to the skyrocketing number of incarcerated Muslim males and females.

So even just by looking at basic development statistics, it is clear that the majority of Cape Town citizens are experiencing wretched lives. But coming to understand the practices of people will reveal the complexity of their lives.

It would reveal that the impact of collapsed infrastructure services such as health, social welfare and education are abiding features of life, and that hunger and lack of food security are majority experiences in Cape Town.

While one might say that criminal behaviour represents personal and family failings to police the boundaries of children's behaviour, this is not where the origins of the problem lie.

Elite political interests are quick to moralise about causes, attributing blame to individuals and people, which, again, as in the case of their attitude to the carnivals, is a tactic that justifies them 'looking away', preventing them from making social justice commitments.

This is precisely the type of behaviour that Allah calls out in *Sūrah al-Mā`ūn* (The Small Kindnesses, Q. 107:V1-7) when Allah declares,

> Have you ever considered [the kind of person] who gives the lie to all moral law?
>
> Behold, it is this [kind of person] that pushes the orphan away,
>
> And feels no urge to feed the needy.
>
> Woe, then, unto those praying ones whose hearts from their prayer are remote
>
> Those who want only to be seen and praised,
>
> And, withal, deny all assistance [to their fellow-men]!

This *surah* (chapter) powerfully underscores the duplicitousness involved in leading an active outer religious life, while at the same time denying Islam's higher moral commitments. The Qur'an condemns such duplicitousness, especially among those who employ tactics of deception and sharp turns of phrase to prevent them from imagining practices that would turn wretched lives into just lives.

The call of this *khuṭbah* is to place the 'wretched of the earth', in all their fulsome humanness, into the centre of our religious imagination, and to go on to establish big and small commitments and practices to build socially just lives for all in this city.

18. GRATITUDE (SHUKR) AND FRIENDSHIP (ṢADAQAH) IN TRANSACTING A 'METAPHYSICS OF ACTIVE PRESENCE' IN THE CITY[1]

It is a truism that the weather plays an influential role in our daily lives; it directly affects our cleanliness and ablution habits, dress, daily commutes, domestic living arrangements, and our time schedules.

It also affects our senses and our aesthetic appreciation: what we eat and how we observe the world, its colours, sights, smells and sounds.

The weather, whether wind, sunshine, cold, drought or rain, affects our immersion in the *ṣibghah* (colouring) of Allah, in other words, the daily hues, colours or influences in which Allah's overwhelming presence manifests in our lives.

We are inspired by Allah's influences, which shape the daily contours of our lives. Allah declares in *Sūrah al-Baqarah* (The Cow, Q. 2:V138):

> [Say: "Our life takes its] hue (colour) from God! And who could give a better hue [to life] than God, if we but truly worship Him?"

This verse underlines the majestic influence of worshipping Allah, who is ever-present in shaping our lives and destinies. Living in Allah's presence means that we are repositories of Allah's divine qualities.

We are imbued with divine qualities such as beauty (*jamāl*), mercy (*raḥmah*), creativity (*ibdāʿ*) and excellence (*iḥsān*). Living in the presence of the divine means making these qualities an active part of our lives, in the big and small aspects of our lives, be it our relations with our body, our interactions with our families and neighbours, or in our educational institutions or working lives.

It is in the relationships that we establish with ourselves, others and the inanimate world that we attain Allah's *ṣibghah,* God's majestic impact on our being. The nature of our relations with each other is as important as the moral activity that we become involved in. In other words, it is how we do what we do, how we relate to other people and our environment, that defines our daily practices.

The prophet Muhammad (peace be upon him) declares in a *ḥadīth* (saying of the prophet), that 'the salvific quality of life lies in human transaction or relations' with others and the world around us.

Human fellowship, taking care of others and displaying compassion towards each other form the fulcrum of our projects in this world and our salvation in the hereafter.

This *khuṭbah* reminds us that showing gratitude (*shukr*) is one of the most important conditioning qualities of our *muʿāmalāt,* our relations and transactions.

Our experiences with the recent drought is an example of gratitude at work. Whereas just a few weeks ago we prayed for rain, today the dam levels are approaching 50%.

---

1 *Khuṭbah* presented at Claremont Main Road Mosque, 6 July 2018.

And now we are struggling with the devastating effects of flooding in the low-lying areas of the city. We are being challenged to extend our compassion to address a situation where the poorest of the poor are hit hardest by rains.

Our adaptations to the drought have taught us many lessons. The drought affected all classes of people of the city, forcing us to adapt to water scarcity, how to use water sparingly, how a city and its people rally together to address an impending human catastrophe.

We refused to be demoralised by impending doom and gloom; instead, we adapted, developed new environmental norms, and importantly, we adopted new behaviours, which have now become lodged in our consciousness.

In addition to a greater awareness of the sustainable and sparing use of water, we have placed ourselves in a position to extend our ethical behaviour to broader ecological concerns, addressing poverty alleviation in the city, and developing fellowship and cooperation around ongoing spatial and other injustices in the city.

We thank Allah for blessing us with the current rains in full awareness of the need to put our gratitude to good use and moral repurposing.

Allah declares in *Sūrah Ibrahīm* (Abraham, Q. 14:V7)

> And when your Sustainer made this promise: "If you are grateful [to Me], I shall most certainly give you more and more; but if you are ungrateful, verily, My chastisement will be severe indeed!

Gratitude for Allah's *ni`am* (favours), being grateful, giving thanks and a disposition of thanksgiving are qualities that stand at the centre of Islam's ethical vision.

In the case of the drought, for us, being grateful to Allah as an ethical disposition has translated into life-affirming practical action.

It is clear that accessing Allah's *ṣibghah,* the hues, or Allah's manifest qualities, lies in translating Allah-ordained dispositions such as mercy, gratitude, creativity and excellence into ethical practices, *a`māl al-ṣālihāt,* that advance the common good.

This *khuṭbah* emphasises the qur'anic view that *shukr,* or gratitude-inspired practices are a sign and expression of living in God's presence.

A *shākir,* or one who is imbued with gratitude, engages in what I call in this *khuṭbah* a ***'metaphysics of active presence,'*** which is an acute awareness of Allah's divinity in our lives, in the way in which we are imbued with the Godly ordained values that manifest in our *akhlāq,* our behaviour and ethical conduct.

The *shākir* (the grateful person) is actively present in life's daily challenges, and responsive to the contingencies of time and place. Laying emphasis on gratitude as a condition of success, the verse cited above also juxtaposes *shukr* with *kufr,* gratitude with ingratitude. It establishes the proposition that *kufr* or ingratitude is the denial of the bounty of Allah.

Kufr or ingratitude is the seedbed of our destruction, negative living, and an ego-centred existence. *Kufr* closes the door on humans' capacity to manifest Allah's mercy, love and compassion.

A *kāfir*, an ingrate, is one who denies or refuses to acknowledge Allah's truth, Allah's manifest qualities, or the creative possibilities that inhere in these qualities. A *kāfir* is never productive, always part of the problem, the one who cuts off other people through rudeness with a negative turn of phrase or attitude, the one who cannot see the full humanness of others.

Kufr or ingratitude is a disposition of *ẕulm* (darkness), causing things to be out of whack, to become dark, or opaque, leading to confusion and demoralisation.

The *mufassir* (exegete) of the Qur'an, Muhammad Asad, eloquently defined the meaning of *kufr* in the Qur'an. Asad explains that the meaning of *kufr* as ingratitude is grasped when we bear in mind that its root verb is '*kafara*', which means to cover up something, a reference to one who denies, or refuses to acknowledge the Truth.

The denial associated with *kufr* refers to denying the Truth in its widest, spiritual sense, whether relating to the existence of God, or to a moral injunction, or to a self-evident moral proposition. Such denial fails to acknowledge and express gratitude for Allah's bounty.

Thus, it is clear that the qur'anic denotation of the word *kufr* means 'denial of truth' and 'ingratitude'. The *kuffār* are all those who are ungrateful in response to the truth of Allah's moral law, and refuse the necessity to establish healthy and productive human conduct.

Our religious and public discourses ought to actively counteract *kufr*. We should expose the 'dead-end street' that accompanies ingratitude, whether in dealing with our domestic circumstances, or with the myriad of social challenges that we confront daily.

The ungrateful drain our emotional energy. Ingratitude accompanies an ego-centred existence, placing the unsatisfied 'self' at the centre of our concerns. *Kufr* or ingratitude never resolves anything, never pushes towards alleviation or human flourishing.

Ingratitude causes us to lapse into a vicious cycle of regret and refusal – refusal to connect ourselves to others or to connect the self to moral and ethical conduct. *Kufr* denies us access to Allah's mercy, compassion and love. A condition of *shukr*, gratitude, in contrast, opens us up to a productive confrontation with humans' earthly existence. At a very simple level, showing gratitude opens us to others, inviting an embrace.

It lays the basis for getting into the 'face' of the other, into the 'face' of strangers, of humans whom we discount, and the complexity and difficulty that we disavow. An Allah-imbued disposition of gratitude breaks down the veil behind which the 'other,' our enemy, lurks. Gratitude allows us to see and touch the 'face of the other', as the philosopher Levinas explains. Gratitude is the key to an active presence in our interactions with others, whose concerns become our concerns. And gratitude also opens us up to embracing those who are hostile towards us.

The Qur'an lays emphasis in numerous verses on touching the face of people, of identifying with their plight, by teaching us about the beauty of establishing friendship, Allah declares in *Sūrah Fuṣṣilat* (Explained in Detail);

> Not equal are the good deed and the bad deed. Repel evil by that which is better, and then the one who is hostile to you will become as a devoted friend (Q. 41:V34).

A *tafsīr* (exegesis) of this verse explains that Allah commands the believers to be patient when we feel angry, to be forbearing when confronted with ignorance, and to forgive when we are mistreated. If we do this, Allah will save us from Satan and subdue our enemies until we become like close friends.

It is therefore the advice (*nasīḥah*) of this *khuṭbah* that we should work to access Allah's mercy and compassion through our attitudes and behaviour towards those closest to us and those whom we may not even know. A disposition of gratitude in the face of challenge and adversity opens the door for us to establish healthy relations, alliances and friendships. Such relations are crucial for adaptation and flourishing.

And our invitation is to place *shukr* or gratitude at the centre of an engaged life in the mercy of the divine. Such a life would allow our daily lives to be imbued with the hues and qualities of Allah's divine grace.

19. AFTER THE VERULAM MOSQUE ATTACK WE NEED TO URGENTLY COUNTER SECTARIAN DISCOURSE IN OUR COMMUNITIES[1]

Changing discourses and perspectives in communities is complex and tough. This is indeed the case with current-day sectarian discourses among Muslims. But discourse, or what and how we choose to talk, also kills.

This has been shown by the recent attack on a Shi`a mosque in Durban. Speculation is that this is a copycat local ISIS-inspired attack, in which case the severe brand of *takfīri* terror has now hit our local shores with devastating effect.

The killing could also be the result of the local anti-Shi`a diatribes that have characterised South African Muslim discourse since the 1980s. Such narcissistic polemics have increased in recent years to frame Shi`as as non-Muslim whose blood is literally *ḥalāl*, i.e. permissible to shed.

This bigotry is unconstitutional and anti-human rights, yet its roots are deep and complex.

It has been allowed to fester and feed Muslim public sentiment and has largely remained unchallenged. South Africa's human rights regime has guaranteed the free existence of heterodox identities, expressed through intra-religious diversity.

However, many groups have found ways to violate such guarantees. These mostly happen in the semi- and informal institutional spaces of communities. And Muslims, like other groups, have been destabilised by such pockets of intolerance.

Hate and whispering campaigns have run freely on social media. Prominent imams and organisations have failed to condemn such anachronistic behaviour, while others have openly promoted hostility and hatred. Left unchecked, this whispering campaign lodges in the minds of people. This results in perpetrators coming to view Shi`as, for example, as less than human.

This plays a key mobilising role when people, who often act from their own complex and sometimes marginalised life perspectives, are persuaded to run a victimisation campaign against people who are framed as 'non-' or 'lesser' Muslims. The consequences, as we witnessed in Durban, are devastating.

What is required is to develop an internal Muslim dialogue that calls out hate speech and violence. Not tolerating hate-mongering and sectarianism is crucial. We have to change the discursive terms of acceptability among people. This must be informed by the politics of the long term, which requires challenging recalcitrant discourses.

It also requires active engagement processes in communities, schools, classrooms, mosque pulpits and our community organisations. This is where complex conversations have to be held, questions posed, and norms of civic cohesion generated.

---

1 First published in in the *Daily Maverick,* 28 May 2018.

Condemning bad behaviour is important, and establishing practices in communities that promote well-rounded behaviour is crucial. But changing our community discourses is a necessary, if not sufficient, condition for turning the tide.

This will take brave men and women, who singly and in unison are able to act principally and strategically to counteract the ransacking of our religion and lifestyles which are geared towards cultivating a capacious civilizational mindset. We need to respond now with fortitude, compassion and care lest we lose our children to the 'fanaticism of ignorance' currently running rampant in our communities.

20. REREADING THE LEGACY OF IMAM HARON IN THE 50TH YEAR OF COMMEMORATING HIS MARTYRDOM[1]

As we enter the 50th year since the tragic passing of Imam Abdullah Haron, the question arises whether we dare to read the Imam's legacy differently and put such a reading to productive work in our current times.

The seed for doing this was planted during the 11th annual Imam Haron Memorial Lecture, which was delivered this year by his son, Prof. Muhammed Haron at the Zohra Noor Auditorium, Islamia College, on 26 September. Muhammed pointed in this direction by offering a nuanced and contemporaneous reading of his father's life.

In the lecture, Prof. Haron combined personal insights with a portrayal of key formative events in the Imam's life. Haron, the son, called for a broader and more incisive range of scholarly work that would bring his father's life into fuller, multidimensional view, which I believe would offer a robust 'reading' of the meaning of such a life for our complex contemporary moment.

Imam Abdullah Haron was born in Claremont on 8 February 1924 and brutally killed by the apartheid regime in prison on 27 September 1969. He was the Imam of the Al-Jaamia Mosque in Stegman Rd, Claremont from 1955 until his death.

The political and broader discursive parameters have changed fundamentally since then, and the Imam's legacy should be mined to allow us to work productively with a fuller and more complex set of human dynamics that characterise our lives in Cape Town and in the world. The impending 50th anniversary commemoration is an apt opportunity to begin this task.

Muhammed Haron correctly and courageously portrayed his father as a 'man for all seasons', a person with a multidimensional personality, a photogenic family man, a great dresser, a brother and father who was actively engaged in the lives of his siblings, who loved his dear wife Galima (nee Sadan), and played a formative role shaping the sensibilities of his three children, Fatiema, Muhammed and Shamila, the latter who settled in the United Kingdom, where she raised her own family.

The Imam was an avid music lover. He had a piano in his house in Crawford and encouraged his children to appreciate music. He was involved in active inter-faith work and encouraged the reading of literature, religious and especially Islamic books, and the English translation of the Qur'an.

There are many photos of the Imam surrounded by his younger congregants. Muhammed Haron explained that his father loved children and young people. A powerful memory for Muhammed was his father's constant recitation of the Qur'an – in other words, a memory of a person who was a *Ḥāfiẓ al-Qur ʿān* (one who memorised the entire Qur'an) and had come to personify its ethical message.

1 In *Cape Argus*, October 2018

The Imam's life was thus accompanied by the Qur'an, and he was motivated in life by its exhortation to fairness and justice. And so, as Muhammed Haron explained, he was always wont to give testimony to the injustices, big and small, which he encountered. It was the injustices associated with racism and apartheid that became the Imam's defining quality, the spiritual fuel that imbued his life with the clarity of moral purpose

The Imam for all seasons was above all a witness bearer for justice as exhorted by the Qur'an, in which his life was immersed. Bearing witness was what gave meaning to his life, and in displaying his commitments in an often questioning and conservative community his example shone like a very bright light.

He was a person ahead of his time, never fully supported by the broader Muslim community or its organisations. This community was mired in living its own accommodations with the brutal apartheid state, turning a blind eye to its repressive machinery, as it tried to maximise some advantage in dire circumstances. Arguably, some prominent people in the Muslim community were compliant supplicants of the apartheid state, collaborators seeking advantage.

Imam Haron's legacy was picked up and celebrated prominently only later by young educated Muslim students and others from the late 1970s. They appropriated his legacy as one of their key mobilising platforms for their activism, in the process correctly emphasising his anti-apartheid legacy and martyrdom.

The other dimensions of his life, including art, reading, family, sport, interfaith solidarity, retail worker and snappy dresser – in other words, the more mundane aspects – may have been underplayed. Offering a reading of his legacy by emphasising these aspects would be a first step which, together with his political commitments, would offer a deeper understanding of Imam Haron's legacy.

In asserting his multidimensional legacy, I believe we ought to have an important conversation about how such a legacy could be put to work in current times. Imam Haron has much to offer us in democratic times, of hopes dashed, a faltering and corrupt state, and multiple human rights tragedies occurring daily.

The Imam's legacy would have much to say about how we as citizens of this country and the world ought to go about establishing a caring, humane and inclusive society. But the route towards such a dispensation depends on us. The Imam's life provides many important clues, but we have to step up to do the intellectual work and activism to make his legacy come alive in novel, inclusive, open-minded and exciting ways in our city, country and the world.

21. SEARCHING FOR IMAM HARON: REFLECTIONS ON RECENT INTRA-MUSLIM POLEMICS IN SOUTH AFRICAN MUSLIM CIVIL SOCIETY SPACE[1]

One has to embrace one's history, one has to engage with it, and most importantly, one has to enter into a productive conversation with it in order to identify how to adapt to the present and future anticipated circumstances. One has to be willing to shed corrosive and redundant practices and go on to establish an engaged and responsive ethical presence in our local contexts.

The presentation today turns on a consideration of Muslims as civil society actors engaged in the public sphere, their place in this sphere and, most importantly, the terms on which they establish their practices in this sphere.

I place the martyrological figure of al-Shahīd Imam Abdullah Haron at the centre of this presentation. I provide the following trope for my presentation; that is, Imam Abdullah Haron presents the impossible as a possibility through his Muslim-inspired praxis during the 1950s and 1960s. And, I suggest that it is time that we place this impossible possibility, in the light of his example, at the centre of our ethical commitments.

But for me the question is how do we do this? Who was Imam Haron? What is the nature of his ethically informed social and political praxis, in other words, how can the significance of his life best be understood and put to use in 2019?

I am using Imam Haron's example as a way of considering what is key to the Cape and South African Muslim community-formation processes, their adaptation, development, co-dependent interaction with other communities, and with the state.

I would like to start by offering a conceptual distinction between community discourse based on *identity* and community discourse based on *ethics*. These two concepts work together, sometimes relatively separately, and sometimes even at cross-purposes in community processes in the light of very specific circumstances.

How identity and ethics come together and are given specific meaning is the outcome of the contingencies of histories and social actors. The relationship between ethics and identity expresses itself differently, for example, in the 1950s and 1960s in the time of Imam Haron, compared to how it works in 2019, in the now.

Identity-based community responses refer to the internal discourses, dramas and the dynamics of the group, kept relatively insulated from the dramas of the outside world. The dramas of the outside world have an impact and play a role, but these are read through the prism of the need to maintain internal group identity cohesion. Language, metaphor and law are mobilised to justify, explain and mediate dynamics internal to the group. The logic of the identity response is always informed by internal argument and justification within the group, never to the outside world.

1 This was a paper presented at the Islamic Peace College South Africa (IPSA), 16 February 2019.

The ethical, in turn, involves a broader commitment to the higher purposes of life. Not to be seen as separate from identity, an ethical stance is founded on the human impulse to act against one's narrow interests, to act with and for others, and to engage in behaviour that secures life for all. Ethics is about the self always connected to others, and in the exigencies of the times connected to animals and inanimate objects, the earth and its survival.

An ethical stance involves less calculation and entails more of a type of selfless behaviour. The ethical involves impulses for social justice such as commanded in the Qur'an's exhortation to stand up for justice, even if against self or kin – another oft-quoted exhortation about Allah conferring dignity on all the progeny of Adam, or in another Quranic verse where Allah (SWT) confers dignity and leadership on the oppressed of the earth.

In the contemporary world, the impulse to the political often trades on and emphasises religion as conferring an identity, whether a primordial Islamic identity or Hindu identity or a Jewish identity, as the primary hallmark or raison d'être of one's existence in the world. Here the focus is on the internal identity dynamics of belonging that constitute a religious or communal identity.

For example, in our case, Islam's public discourses and its credal dramas, whether through Wahhābi, Deobandi, Shāfiʿiyah, Sunni, Barelwi or Sufi credal authority, are the primary frames whereby most Muslims encounter and adapt to the world.

In such a situation the ethical commitment to mutual human interdependence, human rights, dignity, gender equality and our planetary existence in the face of increasing poverty, the impact of climate change, suffering families, collapsing educational infrastructures and food insecurity is a conceptual afterthought, or a secondary conceptual marker, not the primary framing in our conceptual schemata.

These ethical commitments and issues of higher-order *maslaḥah* (common human interests) are either absent in our community repertoires, or we react and respond to them in a kneejerk and incoherent manner. In other words, our Muslim religious communities struggle to establish a meaningful articulation between higher-order ethical framings and narrower identity framings. I argue that we should carefully study history to find out when and under what circumstances greater ethical clarity and purpose overcame narrower religious identity operations and commitments in the community.

And it is here that the martyrological figure of Imam Abdullah Haron is instructive. Imam Haron was an inheritor of the Muslim religious legacy of Shaykh Yusuf, Tuan Guru and Abdol Burns, Abdullah Abdurahman, Fatima Meer and Zainunisa 'Cissie' Gool. Imam Haron's *ʿulāmā* contemporaries were people like his teacher Shaykh Ismail Ganief, and his friends Shaykh Abubakr Najaar, Shaykh Nazeem Mohamed, Dr Abu Bakr Fakir, Boeta Ismail Saban, Boeta Ali Fisher and others.

He was a bearer of both identity and justice. He was a traditional Cape Town imam, young, well dressed, a music and sports lover, a multidimensional family man. He was a *Ḥāfiẓ al-Qurʾān* who loved to recite the Qur'an and he fasted twice a week.

He was the chair of the Muslim Judicial Council from 1959 to 1960 and the honorary editor of the *Muslim News*, in addition to working for Wilson Rowntree. He was a frequent visitor in black African townships, doing *da`wah* (missionary work), spreading the truth of his *dīn*.

And he was an internationalist, a global traveller and a connector of people. He was also part of the activist milieu that emerged in Claremont during the 1950s, where he interacted with young intellectuals during that period. This is where he developed an acute South African-centred ethical consciousness.

He worked in the political underground providing material relief for families of detainees, among others. He was imprisoned for his political activism in May 1969 and died 123 days later on 27 September 1969.

His ethical identification was pure. His refusal to capitulate to discomfort, humiliation and torture emanated from deep within his ethical commitment to the supreme values of love, dignity and justice.

During the brutal repression of the 1960s the only political option available to respond to apartheid was an ethical option. It was a choice of either living a wretched oppressive life or a life in service of liberation which, as his chosen path, led to his death caused by the apartheid regime.

Imam Haron's ethical recognition (*ma`rifah*) led to his death, an apartheid killing to be re-inquested in our country's legal system, hopefully soon. It was a glorious death that affirmed humanity's beautiful existence and gave us life, 50 years after his death. We know that Imam Haron's death was processed largely through the category of identity and the accommodations that Muslims of the time made with the apartheid dispensation.

His funeral was an enormous symbolic statement that saluted the life of this man. But the community's responses largely involved distancing themselves from his politics. The *Muslim News*, of which he was an editor, 5 days later distanced itself from the Imam in its pages, taking the view in writing that if he had died for his political and/or ethical views, the newspaper would distance itself from Imam Haron.

My reading of his life and death is that for one moment in time the community was gifted with an ethical life, ethical clarity and that as a consequence the community for one brief moment shone brightly.

But then the community reverted back to an identity based on internal justification and accommodation to the apartheid dispensation. It was only later that Muslim youth groups picked up the baton from Imam Haron, mobilised in his memory, in an attempt to confer ethical content on their Islamic anti-apartheid commitments.

It is gratifying that recently a broad spectrum of organisations have committed to properly commemorating the 50th anniversary of Imam Haron's death. In my view the challenge in this regard is to establish a proper relationship between identity and ethics, to mobilise religious identity in service of the ethical.

Don't misunderstand me; religious identity is the *sine qua non* of Muslims' community life in Cape Town, and of any religious community for that matter. A religiously inspired life is not by definition cut off from broader moral commitments.

But the proof of this is in the pudding: the proper relationship between the ethical and the political is the stuff of careful reflection on our everyday religious and community practices.

In a previous paper, my colleague and I (see Bangstad and Fataar 2010) called this tussle between the ethical and the political, between broader commitments to humanity and narrower commitments to community and identity, an 'ambiguous accommodation'. This is the idea that the Muslim community, with its many different social, class, gender, cultural, ethnic and transnational fragments, has established a kind of ambivalent identity, one that is powerfully framed by an inwardness, relatively doubtful of the outside secular world, and a strategic embrace of the democratic space, an assertion of our identity and place in the world. We could thus say that our community responses and practices fall between narrow commitments to self-preservation and the need for broader alliances and broader challenges.

Let me give you three current-day examples of this ambivalence, each example showing a particular manifestation of this ambiguous accommodation. My aim in purposefully offering these examples is to provoke debate. I want to show how the ethical might be obscured by narrow identity assertions.

The first example is the Bo-Kaap anti-gentrification campaign. This is highly laudable, courageous and timely. And we are all participating in it. This campaign has brought sharply to the fore the spatial injustice in the urban core and the suffering of historically located communities in their desperate attempts to retain this space as their cultural heritage.

The Bo-Kaap campaign would manifest greater solidarity if connections were to be made conceptually and physically to spatial justice campaigns all over the country and to similar and different struggles in places such as Tafelsig, Witsand, Parkwood, Langa and Bonteheuwel to connect with refugee communities, black African spatial struggles, the homeless, and so on. Cultural preservation, informed by an assertion of identity, would form part of larger spatial justice struggles by people acting in solidarity with one another in the city, the country and the globe.

The second example centres on the debacle generated largely by social media and populist responses over the ceremony that followed the marriage between two persons.

My impression is that the proverbial shite hit the fan over two things, the one preceding the other; one was a shameful misunderstanding of the correctness of the marriage as a result of questioning the reversion to Islam of the bridegroom, and the second over the ceremony afterwards. Social media created and accentuated the '*fietnah*' (creating falsities via local grapevine-type gossip).

This situation was provoked by crude populist responses circulating on Facebook. In my understanding, it was this vilification or '*fietnah*' that provided the impetus for the Muslim Judiciary to step in. The MJC probably felt it had no option but to deal with the issue so as to bring clarity and sanity to the matter, instead of allowing the matter to run out of control.

But actually, the matter, framed as it had been by populist *fietnah* on social media, had already run beyond control. What followed was reactive, and it is perhaps important to reflect on the responses.

My comments here will not deal with the merits of the MJC's ruling or position taken in response but will address some aspects of the methodology by which the response was made.

I am particularly interested in how the two concepts of ethics and identity played themselves out in the management of this incident, and to draw a larger lesson about the way our Muslim civic responses are currently working.

I suggest to you that the MJC's response was resolved primarily through the lenses of intra-religious identity discourses, not through ethical lenses.

I must insist that there is a history to any response; the nature of any response is partly but powerfully informed by the preceding discourses around the response. Am I suggesting that I could have guessed how this was going to play out once we understood how this issue became a religious problem? Perhaps. Although people, positions and arguments still had to be mobilised to dress up the response in a particular way.

The religious language mobilised notions of *shirk* (idolatry), *kufr* (unbelief) and *ḥarām* (unlawful) as the conceptual window through which to process the incident. The judiciary found that the fire circulations during the ceremony were deemed to be *haram*.

But let me put this to you; what was never in play in processing the response was the ethical dimension. The response was not arrived at through equal, proper and rigorous consideration of the potential impact of living in a plural multi-faith, multi-cultural secular democracy. The ethics of coexistence and co-living might indeed have been in play during the processing. After all, we live in democratic South Africa. But this ethical stance is nowhere to be found in the actual position taken.

The position adopted and announced was entirely driven by narrow parochial religious interests. It is not as if an ethical position on this matter could not be sustained in a *sharʿī* (Islamic legal) argument. It was simply that the ethical may never properly have been brought into the deliberations.

The judiciary's position was produced from an identity-oriented perspective, not on the basis of an ethics of co-existence and mutual interdependence.

The response was provoked by the populism and rantings of people on social media. And my reading of the incident is that the judiciary's response was an attempt to mollify this populism, in the process giving narrow identity concerns pride of place.

There was an attempt to put everyone on the backfoot, hence the call for an apology. But no one asked key ethically informed questions such as:

- What are the symbolic / religious meanings of these so-called Hindu practices? Can a religious ritual be emptied of its religious content and presented as simply ceremonial? Isn't intention pivotal in action?
- Has the Hindu-inspired *rampies-sny* ceremony at the celebration of the birth of the Prophet not been emptied of its Hindu religious symbolism? Ditto for the *mendhi* celebrations before an Indian Muslim wedding. Does a Hindu ritual's appropriation into a wedding ceremony imply a religious / *fiqh* infraction, even *shirk* or *ḥarām*? It is commendable that the MJC distanced itself from calling the event *shirk* or *kufr*.

- What is *shirk*? What is the historically contingent context for *shirk* in 7th-century Arabia and how should the quranic position on *shirk* be understood in the contingent context of 7th-century Arabia?
- How has the doctrine of *shirk* emerged and developed in the Islamic intellectual tradition across 14 centuries? How, for example, have power and politics in places like India and Pakistan impacted on debates on *shirk* discourses in the context of the politics of Hindutva?
- What are the different forms of *shirk* and what does one think of *shirk* in the 21st century?
- Is the concept of divinity in Hinduism tantamount to *shirk*? Why? Analogously, the Qur'an calls out Christian belief in the Trinity as a form of *shirk*, but Muslim relations with Christians, interestingly, are based on their status as '*Ahl al-Kitāb*' (People of the Book).
- Should we not at the very least have given ourselves space to educate ourselves properly on these matters? Should we not have engaged directly with Hindu religious experts and academic specialists on these matters? Why did we all run to Mullah Google for answers to these complex and intricate matters? Should we not have attempted to mollify and educate the populists in our community?

In the logic of my presentation today, the adopted position was entirely processed through an assertion of the hermeneutics of identity. An educational, philosophical and research-orientated hermeneutic would have brought the ethical response informed by human existence into view, at the very least. By bringing ethics into the discussion, we would have given ourselves the opportunity to consider larger ethical questions related to our everyday lives in this city and the world.

The third example requires more time to explain, but let me give a truncated view of the call by our black African Muslim compatriots for identity recognition as authentically Muslim. This issue speaks to the nature of our religious identification. A group of black African Muslims is organising a blacks-only Muslim conference in Soweto in March 2019.

Some are objecting, arguing that Islam does not condone racism and that organising a conference on the basis of race is in itself a violation of Islam. Really? In what world are we living?

The trope of African Muslims in this country being discriminated against by some in the Indian and coloured Muslim communities comes a long way. African Muslims experience racism in the workplace, in the organisation of mosques, about who can lead, who cleans, who controls the money, etc. They correctly feel violated when a mosque's Trust deed says 'only Indians can be trustees of this mosque'.

Why can these mosques not change their Trust deeds to potentially and actually include anyone on its Trust, and concomitantly, also change exclusionary behaviour toward African Muslims? This is a clear case of negative religious identity still asserting itself in our community. Identity clearly trumps ethicality in this example.

In conclusion, Imam Haron's exemplary life shows acutely the struggle between identity and ethics. Imam Haron seamlessly lived the identity of a proud Muslim imbued with an ethical *rūḥ* (spirit). This spirit accorded him the impulse to perfectly recognise his commitment to dignity, love and justice. This commitment led to his martyrdom, which gave beautiful life to all of us.

I argue that his life was imbued with the ethical, the ethics of the Qur'an, and it was through the ethical that he mobilised his religious identity in the service of the higher purposes of our human existence. This, I would argue, is what we should retrieve from Imam Haron's martyrdom in the 50th year of its commemoration.

REFERENCE

Bangstad, S. and Fataar, A. 2010. Ambiguous Accommodation: Cape Muslims and Post-Apartheid Politics. *Journal of Southern African Studies*, 36, (4): 817-831.

22. THE LIVING ROLE OF THOSE WHO DIED FOR US TO BE FREE[1]

> And say not of those who are slain in the path of God's cause.
> "They are dead". Nay, they are alive though you perceive it not.
> (*Surah al-Baqarah,* The cow, Q. 2:154)

This qur'anic verse provides one very important way to productively work with the personal, social and political meanings of martyrdom. We should ask how is the martyr alive today?

First, we need to ask permission from the families to speak about their martyred sons and daughters, as these families are burdened by their ongoing search for justice.

The answer we give about the living martyrs among us, as the verse exhorts, is the suggestion that they live among us in the ethical sense, in the idea that their death gives life to the higher values and purposes of life: *ḥurriyyah* (freedom), *ʿadl* (justice), *karāmah* (dignity) and *salām,* which is the existential condition of peace.

The martyr is alive in the ethical content that we give to our human endeavours. *Shuhadā* or witness-bearing forces a productive conversation between the ethical, our commitment to justice, freedom and dignity, on the one hand, and our political behaviour in everyday life, on the other.

The imperative to bear witness impels us to establish a political path towards justice. The political, legal and juridical are democracy's instruments available for use towards establishing justice in the service of the greater good.

The political engages the contingencies of the here and the now – corruption, state capture, inequality and underdevelopment, and human indignities suffered in the context of large-scale poverty.

The political is the art of the possible, currently given expression in the fight over the vote, and considerations over which party to vote for. Voting is a necessary, but not sufficient condition in a democracy, a way of calling in people's hopes and desires, and thereby giving them a stake in our shared public futures and co-existence.

Politics, however, is always informed by the ethical demands made on it by the figure of the martyr who lives among us and comes alive, to an even greater extent, in conditions of deprivation.

Martyrdom forces our collective imaginary to search for and connect the political to a productive ethical path. The blood of the martyr nourishes us on such a journey and ties us firmly to our search for freedom and peace. This is the litmus test posed

---

1 The piece is based on comments at the Freedom symposium, Spice Mecca Ramaḍān Expo, Cape Town Castle, 27 April 2019. These comments were made in response to presentations by family members of martyred heroes of the struggles, slain by the apartheid government, including Imam Abdullah Haron, Steve Biko, Ahmed Timol and Fort Calata.

by the martyr; the blood of the martyr keeps our feet firmly to the fire. It is only those political expressions that can tie the political firmly, confidently and courageously to the ethical purposes of life that deserve our vote.

The deathly life of the martyr among us would be wasted on a politics tied to spatial injustice in this city and our country. This is particularly so in the context of this Castle from where colonialism and its burdens were spread, creating what was yesterday referred to by Ebrahim Rasool as a '*dār al-la`nah,* an accursed abode.

The blood of the martyr would be wasted on those who support the Zionist state of Israel in its persecution of the Palestinians, on those who trample on the sovereignty of Venezuela, on those who fail to be hospitable to the refugee, on those who fail to challenge gender inequities and all other forms of discrimination, and on those who violate the dignity and human rights of the farmworker, the factory worker and the township dweller.

`Adl or justice comes to fruition only when the political pathway is imbued with the crystal clarity of the martyr who is alive among us, though we perceive it not.

23. FROM ABSTINENCE (IMSĀK) TO ELEVATION (RIFʿAH): REIMAGINING IMAM ABDULLAH HARON'S PATH OF SHAHĀDAH (BEARING WITNESS) IN THE QUEST FOR JUSTICE AND DIGNITY[1]

Imam Abdullah Haron's life and martyrdom present the Muslim community of Cape Town with an opportunity and a challenge. The opportunity resides in putting his example to proper use as an ethical inspiration for life in 2019 and beyond. The challenge lies in how we put the figure of Imam Haron to use and to what version of his life we choose to give prominence.

This is an urgent yet precarious task. In this *khuṭbah* today I present an engaged ethical reading based on advice that I take from the Prophet Muhammad (peace be upon him) which he gave when one of his companions came to him to ask about the path to righteousness. The Prophet replied,

> Consult your heart. Righteousness is that about which your soul feels at ease and the heart feels tranquil (transmitted by Aḥmad ibn Ḥanbal and al-Dārimī).

Reimagining the righteous life of Imam Haron, whose soul is at ease and whose heart is tranquil, is based on a reading of the literature on his life and his killing by the apartheid government.

Having absorbed the details, I have come to the conclusion that one has to render an understanding based on a type of heart reading, not simply rational readings. Such a rendition of a worthy life must account for all the dimensions that make up his life and martyrdom.

Consulting your heart, as the Prophet suggests, is based on a reading in which Allah's divine grace is at the centre of the righteous life of the martyr (*shahīd*). Such a rendition would bring us closer to what Allah explains to us in the Qur'an:

> And say not of those who are slain in God's cause, "They are dead": nay, they are alive, but you perceive it not. (Q. 2:V154)

The martyr's example comes to life in the ethical connections that we make as we attempt to imbue our lives with dignity, fairness and justice.

Considering how to put Imam Haron's martyrdom to ethical use comes alive in a conversation with our community's past, and the Imam's story as a foundational part of this conversation.

Imam Haron was an inheritor of a long line of men and women whose lineage is traced from all over the world, especially the Indonesian archipelago, West and East Africa, Mozambique, Madagascar and India, encompassing local Free Blacks, and

1 *Khutbah* delivered at Claremont Main Road Mosque, 31 May 2019.

various indigenous connections made under conditions of colonial harshness and brutality at the Cape.

The impact of Allah's divine intervention was at play when communities and families fashioned themselves out of the raw materials of a brutal existence under conditions of exile, banishment and slavery.

Imam `Abdullah ibn Qādī 'Abd al-Salām, the celebrated imam known as 'Tuan Guru', who established the first *madrasa* in the Cape on land bequeathed as *waqf* (religious endowment) by the freed slave woman, Saartjie van der Kaap (1775-1847), described this city upon his banishment and imprisonment on Robben Island as a '*dār al- ḥuzn*', a depressive place of deprivation.

The nascent community used its Islamically informed ethos to domesticate the harsh environment by deploying community-building processes that helped them establish a viable existence on the edges of the colonial city.

Some of their inventiveness involved writing the Qur'an from memory and *kutub* (religious texts) in Afrikaans written in the Jawi-Arabic script, the linguistic form that they invented. The community was strengthened by spiritual ritual practices, celebrations and commemorations that gave it cohesion and an ethic of self-reliance.

Imam Abdullah Haron was formed by this community's social and religious cohesiveness from the time he was born in 1924. He was immersed in its liturgical '*gadāt*' practices and the socio-cultural rhythms of his people.

His God-consciousness was generated by intense personal commitment through participating in the spiritual cultivation of his community, which had practised the remembrance of Allah in the *Rātibul Ḥadād* liturgy from the earliest times of the settlement.

Their spiritual cultivation practices were based on an instruction to the faithful in the Qur'an, (*Surah Al-Imran*, The Family of Imrān, Q. 3:V73), when Allah declares,

> Human beings said to them: "A great army is gathering against you":
> And frightened them: But it (only) increased their Faith: They said:
> "For us Allah is sufficient, and He is the best disposer of affairs.

True faith in and commitment to Allah, enacted through the bodily practices of the believer, through steadfast prayer and fasting, provided the biotechnologies or spiritual tools in respect of which the *ḥuzn* or the depressive colonial state was conquered.

It is no coincidence that Imam Haron fasted throughout his adult life on a Monday and Thursday, following the Prophet's example, and as a *Ḥāfiẓ al-Qur`ān* (one who memorised the Qur'an) he constantly recited verses of the text, as a way of fortifying him on his life path.

Muḥyī al-Dīn ibn `Arabī (1126-1214), the great Sufi mystic and scholar from Al Andalus, explains that fasting affords the one who fasts an elevation to Allah, what is called '*rif`ah*', The fast, according to him is,

> … an abstinence (*imsāk*) whereby those who fast are granted an elevation (*rif`ah*) unto Allah the Most High, and are thus raised above

> all those things from which they have been ordered by al-Haqq (the Divine Law) to distance their souls and limbs (Ibn `Arabī, the translation by Gilis 1999).

Abstinence and elevation are the cornerstones of Imam Abdullah Haron's life. His was a spiritual body cultivated in the disciplining practice of fasting, prayer, recitation and *adhkār* (practices of Divine remembrance) that infused him with a beautiful fearless quality.

Fasting developed the Imam's spiritual body into a body imbued with mental and physical strength, cultivated by his ongoing practices of spiritual elevation that would imbue the martyr, at the opportune moment, with a state of *fiṭrah* or human perfectibility.

Rif`ah or spiritual elevation finds heightened expression in Imam Haron's choice to fast during his imprisonment. We are told that the Imam consciously chose to fast during his incarceration.

With his body, mind and spirit then already disciplined by years of personal tutorship, the relation between abstinence and elevation was now taken to an even higher state of spiritual perfectibility, bringing the time of his *shahādah,* his witness-bearing, into stark reality.

An elevated state of fasting accompanied Imam Haron through his path of imprisonment towards his state of *shahādah,* to finally enter Allah's divine presence as a being who lived the ultimate principled commitment to a life in service of humanity.

Allah explains such an elevation in the Qur'an, *Surah Ibrahīm* (Abraham, Q. 14:V5) as the destination of those who are wholly patient and deeply grateful to God:

> Verily, in this (reminder) there are messages indeed for all who are wholly patient in adversity and deeply grateful [to God].

While suffering incarceration, Imam Haron drank from the spiritual fuel that his perfectible disposition, his *fitrah,* and his belief in Allah provided him. His state of elevation enabled him to remain entirely disciplined and focused on facing adversity in prison.

Imam Haron was arrested on 28 May 1969, the annual day of the celebration of Prophet Muhammad's (peace be upon him) birthday, after being hounded, spied on, followed around and intimidated by the security police for months.

He was detained for his underground work in the struggle against apartheid. He did crucial relief work among the families of detainees and became centrally involved in the underground political activities of the liberation organisations that he was active in during the brutally repressive times of the 1960s.

Imam Haron turned his revulsion at racism into a cultivated anti-apartheid gaze expressed from the Islamic perspective of a traditionally trained Imam.

Some of his writings, for example, used the story of Bilal, a son of a black Abyssinian slave woman, to illustrate the revulsion Islam had for divisions based on colour. Bilal's elevation by the Prophet (peace be upon him) to the highest social rank was proof of Islam's attitude to non-discrimination. Imam Haron loved to use the story of Bilal in his lectures and sermons.

He must have felt acutely the impact of apartheid's laws on his congregants and their stunted life chances. He identified with the indignities visited upon families during their forced removals and the ongoing suffering of those who lived in the harsh living conditions of the city's townships.

Unlike most other imams in Cape Town, he was politically influenced by the restless younger people in his congregation and the broader Claremont community, and it was in this context that he mapped his political and ethical commitments onto his Islamic identity.

His was an Islamic ethical identity seamlessly imbued with clarity of purpose and uncompromising commitment, and it is this heightened attitude that accompanied him during his imprisonment.

Imam Haron was tortured relentlessly. Barney Desai and Cardiff Marley described in their book, *The Killing of the Imam* (1978), how he experienced various phases and forms of torture; softening up, keeping him in the Roeland Street goal and then at the Maitland police station, and then in mid-September 1969, brutally torturing him close to the point of death for three days and nights in a building somewhere in the Cape Town central business district, before returning him to the Maitland police station.

Imam Haron was prevented from changing his clothes, and from getting proper medical treatment. Alas, he gave nothing away. The record shows that he did not give his torturers a single name and no information about any of his underground activities.

Imam Haron had been in a state of heightened elevation during his incarceration, a path for which he had prepared his entire life, mapped as it was onto the spiritual inheritance of his religious forebears. He is an acute example of this spiritual inheritance. He identified with the patience and forbearance of his people in an earlier period and their erstwhile community-building processes.

The ethical coordinates of these earlier community processes, however, had become entangled in the modernising and accommodation-seeking processes of the Cape Muslim community.

Imam Haron understood his community's acquiescence during apartheid. He was, however, never constrained by such an attitude. Instead, he mobilised his spiritual and ethical resources to walk a brave path towards martyrdom relatively parallel to his community.

His was the path that conferred dignity on all the oppressed in this country. His was the path of *shahādah,* a path of bearing witness to Allah, even against oneself, one's kin and those closest to one (based on Qur'an 4, Verse 35).

In a fictionalised, yet apt, account of the last moments of Imam Haron's life, Desai and Marney wrote that,

> Death beckoned and he must prepare. He could die with honour; he had remained a member of the faithful all his life; he had met all

> his obligations to Islam; he had struggled to serve his people and his congregation with all his will and energy; he had kept his word to his comrades, their secret would die with him. Painfully and methodically the Imam undressed. [...] Symbolically he splashed himself with water from his mug. Slowly he donned his pyjamas. He arranged his prayer-mat carefully and, through the blur of pain in his chest, stomach and legs, he knelt in the direction of Mecca and prayed. He prayed for what seemed a long time [...] He folded his prayer mat lovingly and picked up his Qur'an, kissed it and placed it neatly on the folded prayer-mat. Then he lay down on his blankets, placing a hand upon his stomach. ... He rested his head on his other hand and, thus settled and ready to die honourably, murmured a last prayer; "In the name of Allah, the most gracious, the most merciful, forgive me my sins. Please care for my wife and children. Now more than ever they need your guidance and protection. Oh most merciful one, you are the only one, this I believe. And the Prophet Muhammad is your messenger. May peace be on his soul. [...] Oh merciful one, take my soul; [...] forgive my weakening. Oh merciful one, let me die now; let my soul be free; let my people be free." (Desai and Marney 1978, 144-145)

And then al-Shahīd Imam Abdullah Haron was no longer, at least not in the physical sense. 123 days of confinement, abuse, insult, persecution, torture and terror ended for him on that morning of Saturday, 27 September 1969.

The *shahīd* (martyr) enters Allah's divine embrace as a person who lived an exemplary ethical life. In his martyrdom, Imam Abdullah Haron offers us life, an example of an ethical life for us to emulate in our circumstances. In turn, Allah invites the martyr into paradise with this sublime invitation (*Sūrah al-Fajr*, The Dawn, Q. 189:127-130);

> (To the righteous soul will be said:) "O (thou) soul, in (complete) rest and satisfaction! Come back thou to thy Lord,- well pleased (thyself), and well-pleasing unto Him. Enter thou, then, among My devotees! Yea, enter thou My Heaven!

REFERENCES

'Ibn `Arabī. *Secrets of the Heart* (translated by C.A. Gilis, 1999), Beirut, Dar Al-Bouraq.

Desai, B. and Marney C, 1978. *The killing of the Imam.* London, Quartet Books. (Republished by Imam Abdullah Haron Education Trust, 2012)

AFTERWORD

The essays in this book are demonstrations of the practice of Public Theology. Public Theology investigates the public contents of religious faith, the public rationality and reasonableness of religious faith, and the public meaning and significance of religious faith. In this book Prof. Aslam Fataar is practising Public Theology and Ethics from an Islamic perspective. He makes this point clear in the introduction: "In one way or the other, our attempt to tie Islam to democracy, pluralism and justice informs all the chapters in the book" (p. 12).

Public Theology advances three features that religious faiths are to adhere to. These features constitute the acid test for healthy religious beliefs and practices, for religion that is good news to society.

Religion is healthy and good news for society if it emphasises that the reverence and respect for God, and the honour and worship of God are accompanied by the quest for the wellbeing and dignity of all humans and all of creation. This dignity is constituted by a life of healing of all wounds, embracing justice, responsible freedom and equality through equity. In all spheres of life this dignity is acknowledged, affirmed and actualised. These spheres include political life, economic life, ecological life, civil society with all its institutions and individuals, public discourse, public opinion-formation and public policymaking.

The second feature of healthy religion, of religion that makes constructive contributions to society, is that it resists anti-intellectualism. Healthy religion embraces rationality, reasonableness and intellectual analysis of religious beliefs and practices. Healthy religion proclaims that it is not necessary to commit intellectual suicide in order to be a religious believer. Attempts are made to make religious beliefs and practices rationally accessible to those inside and those outside the community of faith. This intellectual character of religion also ensures that religions embrace the complexity of life and that they do not participate in the flight from complexity that we often see. Complexity has various features, namely plurality, ambiguity, ambivalence, paradoxality, duality, tragedy as well as *aporia*, i.e. dead-end street situations. Whilst addressing complexity, Public Theology does not want to hide in vagueness. Public Theology seeks simplicity on the other side of complexity, simplicity that has wrestled with complexity.

The third dimension of healthy religion, which serves the so-called Common Good, is the ethos of tolerance and embrace that healthy religion nurtures. Healthy religion guards against both relativism and absolutism. A lifestyle of extreme relativism implies that we believe in nothing, we stand for nothing, we live for nothing, nothing is right, nothing is wrong. Relativists embrace nihilism. Absolutism implies that I believe dogmatically in my own position and that of my group. There is no room for other positions. Those who differ from me are stereotyped, stigmatised, demonised and eventually annihilated. In this context tolerance is proclaimed, tolerance which means *tolere*, carry each other amidst differences. Related to this positive tolerance, which is more than just simply bearing with the nuisance, is the notion of embrace.

An ethos of embrace proclaims that amidst differences and even past enmity, we reach out to each other and seek life together with each other.

The Public Theology and Ethics in the pages of this book advance a life of dignity for all. It demonstrates the worth and value of intellectual reflection from a religious perspective. It fosters an ethos of tolerance and embrace. These essays seek a life of dignity in all walks of life. The rich variety of public themes bears witness to this.

To publish this book from an Islamic perspective in the Beyers Naudé Centre on Public Theology Series celebrates the rich heritage of inter-religiosity in South African society. People from various religious and secular beliefs worked together to overcome apartheid. Now we can work together to make poverty, unemployment, inequality, violence, social pathologies, state capture and corruption history. This book also honours the legacy of Dr Beyers Naudé, who embraced a life of ecumenicity and inclusion in search of dignity for all.

Prof. Nico Koopman

Vice-Rector; Social Impact, Transformation and Personnel

13 August 2019

www.ingramcontent.com/pod-product-compliance
Lightning Source LLC
Chambersburg PA
CBHW080546090426
42734CB00016B/3213
* 9 7 8 1 9 2 8 3 1 4 6 1 5 *